The Story of Baseball

The story of baseball is packed with unforgettable moments, colorful personalities, explosive rivalries and feuds, tense pennant races and World Series. In this lively book, generously illustrated with photographs, John Rosenburg recalls the prominent highlights of this exciting game, tracing the gradual growth and development of major-league baseball through the past hundred years.

Landmark
Giant

Random House New York

The Story of Baseball

Illustrated with photographs

By John M. Rosenburg

1974 Edition
© Copyright 1972, 1968, 1966, 1964, 1962 by John M. Rosenburg

Photograph credits: Bettmann Archive, pages 10, 11; Brown Brothers, ii-iii, 19, 42, 45
(upper right), 49, 50 (bottom), 55, 57 (bottom), 109, 121 (bottom); Chicago White Sox,
40 (bottom); Culver Pictures, 8, 15, 17, 23, 25, 29, 30, 35, 37, 40 (top), 45 (upper
left), 59, 61, 66, 73, 93, 96; European Picture Service, 45 (bottom), 46, 50 (top), 52
(both), 57 (top), 58, 63, 64, 74, 77, 86 (bottom), 123; New York *Daily News*, 68, 70,
80, 83, 89 (both), 105, 113 (top), 115, 116, 127, 136; Pittsburgh Pirates, 82; United
Press International, 2, 4 (both), 5, 78, 109 (bottom), 111, 126, 128 (top), 130, 137, 140,
143, 146, 149, 156, 158, 159, 161, 164, 165, 167, 170, 171, 175, 179, 180, 181; Wide
World, 71, 81, 86 (top), 91 (both), 92, 95, 99, 100 (both), 102 (both), 108, 110, 128
(right), 131, 135, 138, 141, 144, 148, 150, 154, 160, 169, 177, 178, 183, 184. End-
paper photograph from Culver Pictures.

Cover photographs: Front panel—left top and bottom, Klein & Peters, N.Y. *Daily News*
Color Studio; right top and center, Marvin E. Newman; bottom right, George Heyer.
Back panel—Frank Worth.

Library of Congress Cataloging in Publication Data
Rosenburg, John M.   The story of baseball.
(Landmark giant [4])
SUMMARY: Traces the history, ups and downs, and outstanding
moments of baseball from its beginnings as a unique American sport to the present.
1. Baseball—History—U. S.   [1. Baseball—History]   I. Title.
GV863.A1R6 1972   796.357'09   72-1126
ISBN 0-394-81677-3   ISBN 0-394-91677-8 (lib. bdg.)

Who, above all, should know the stirring tales of the great Ruth and Johnson, DiMaggio and Feller? Who, but the young of today...and the young of all the tomorrows?

While this book, then, was written for boys and girls everywhere, I dedicate it with deepest affection to one youngster in particular—my son, John J., who was twelve when the manuscript was completed.

Acknowledgments

It took about three years to complete the manuscript for *The Story of Baseball*. Naturally, when the last period was struck, I was quite pleased with myself. And yet I realized full well that I could not possibly have assembled so much material and sustained my efforts over so long a period without a great deal of assistance. I would like, therefore, to express my deepest appreciation for this wealth of invaluable aid, which came from many sources and in many forms.

I am especially grateful to the hundreds of sports-loving writers who, for more than a century, so carefully and enthusiastically chronicled the birth and growth of baseball. Without their works to draw from, I could not have established the foundation for this book.

While I read some 35 books covering various aspects of baseball, as well as scores of magazines and newspaper articles, I found the following to be the most helpful:

Baseball by Robert Smith; *America's National Game* by A. G. Spalding; *A Ball Player's Career* by Adrian Constantine Anson; *100 Years of Baseball* and *Hot Stove League* by Lee Allen; *General "Baseball" Doubleday* by Robert S. Holzman; *Ball, Bat and Bishop* by Robert W. Henderson; *Richter's History and Records of Baseball* by Francis C. Richter; *The Babe and I* by Mrs. George Herman Ruth; *Connie Mack* by Fred Lieb; *The Real McGraw* by Mrs. John McGraw; *Baseball's Famous First Basemen* and *Baseball's Famous Pitchers* by Ira Smith; *Gas House Gang and a Couple of Other Guys* by Roy Stockton; *The Yankee Story* by Tom Meany; *Baseball* by Harold Seymour; *The History of Baseball* by Allison Danzig and Joe Reichler.

Source material, of course, is but one of the props a writer must lean on as he labors to put a book-length story together. From a variety of people he needs advice and counsel, coöperation, an understanding of a journalist's problems, and even such things as top-flight typing and proof-reading help. Above all, he needs encouragement.

On all of these counts, I was most fortunate. At the outset, for example, I was lucky enough to receive direction and guidance from Lee Allen, historian of the National Baseball Hall of Fame. And as the manuscript grew, Richard G. Harris, a longtime friend—and a writer and editor of uncommon ability—went over my work and made a number of important suggestions.

During my long experience as a sports writer, however, I learned that prose style alone does not endear one to the baseball fan—a fellow who wants all the key facts and figures and wants them to be correct. In addition, the flavor of any incident under discussion has to be just so. To cover myself in this area, I imposed on two people I can best identify —and with some pride—as baseball fans. The genuine kind. They are Messrs. Frank Dugan and Frank Pacifico.

To all of these gentlemen and to the several others who contributed to this modest effort, I again give my thanks.

J.M.R.

The Story of Baseball

2

EXCITEMENT IN NEW YORK

On the cool, sunny afternoon of October 16, 1969, a man stood in the approximate center of Shea Stadium in New York City and with a triumphant flourish caught a small, white ball that had been lofted toward him from a spot some 250 feet away. Immediately, the thousands of baseball fans who packed the stadium leaped to their feet with a thunderous roar. Hundreds scrambled from their seats and rushed down to the playing area. There, housewives, children and grown men tore chunks of grass from the earth, set off flares and firecrackers, fought over equipment left on the field and painted signs on the stadium walls.

But the joyous frenzy of the moment was not limited to the delirious crowd at Shea Stadium. Millions more, who had been staring at their television sets or listening to their radios, also knew about that history-making catch. And, like the "live" audience, they too responded with electrifying suddenness.

In Manhattan, heart of New York City, for example, thousands poured from homes and offices into the city's streets. In many areas, the crowds on the pavement brought traffic to a complete halt.

Others remained indoors, tearing paper into shreds and hurling it from windows. For a while it looked as if snow had come early to the city. In some places, the paper was knee deep.

People in the streets danced, sang, paraded and wept with joy. Two men sat atop mailboxes on the corner of Madison Avenue and 40th Street, alternately drinking from bottles of champagne and squirting passers-by with the bubbly liquid.

(Above) The triumphant Mets run for safety. (Left) Cleon Jones makes the famous catch that cinched the Series for the Mets.

What was all the excitement about?

A baseball game—the final game of the 1969 World Series, played between the New York Mets of the National League and the Baltimore Orioles of the American League. It ended when Met outfielder Cleon Jones made the catch that gave the Mets a 5–3 victory and clear title to America's baseball championship. The catch had given them their fourth win in five series games.

The unbounded joy that swept New York that mid-October day of 1969 (and the contrasting gloom that pervaded Baltimore, home of the Orioles) is nothing new to Americans. It's the sort of thing that happens every year at World Series time.

A stranger to the United States might well wonder at this state of affairs.

"After all," he could be expected to say, "it's only a *game*."

But baseball is more than a mere game to most Americans. It's a National Pastime. And here is the story of how this came about.

1. A New Game for a New Country

In a single baseball season, as many as 35 or 40 million spectators pay admission to sit in ball parks, where they watch professional or amateur players battle for team honors. Many millions of additional fans follow the games by radio and television. And another 10 million adults and boys participate in organized amateur baseball programs that are not in any way connected with public or private schools.

When one thinks about the enormous popularity of baseball, a pertinent question often comes to mind:

Where did this great national game begin?

Actually the origins of baseball are somewhat hazy. Except for box scores, very little about baseball was recorded before 1900. A great many people insist that baseball is a purely American game invented in 1839 by Abner Doubleday in Cooperstown, New York. Others argue that baseball evolved from the British games of rounders and cricket. The controversy was at its hottest during the early 1900s.

One of the earliest champions of the rounders theory was Henry Chadwick. Born in England in 1824, Chadwick moved to the United States when he was just thirteen years old. Six years later he began a remarkable writing career, covering baseball games for the biggest newspapers and magazines of his day. He also wrote books about baseball for boys and girls, originated the baseball scoring system, compiled the first rule book, and made many other suggestions.

Because he was such an authority, many people referred to Chadwick as the "Father of Baseball." But Chadwick, of all people, refused to agree that baseball originated in America. "The similarity of baseball and rounders is fully identified," he said. "And rounders was played in England two centuries before its appearance in America."

The rounders theory is supported by two books. The first one, *The Boy's Own Book,* was published in London in 1829. In it appeared the rules for rounders. The second book, *The Boy's and Girl's Book of Sports,* was published in America in 1835. The author of the second book obviously copied the first book when describing the rules of the game. But he didn't call it rounders. Instead the game was identified as Base or Goal Ball.

Albert Goodwill Spalding, one of professional baseball's founding fathers, refused to go along with the rounders theory. In fact he called it sheer nonsense. And he formed a committee of baseball notables to settle "once and for all" the matter of baseball's origins. Abraham G. Mills, former president of the National League, was chairman. The group labored for three years before reaching, in 1907, a twofold decision. Baseball had its origin, they announced, in the United States. The first scheme for playing baseball was devised by Abner Doubleday at Cooperstown in 1839.

Who was this Abner Doubleday? And on what had the Mills Commission based its findings?

Doubleday, dead at the time the report was issued, was a well-known Union Army general. He was also a friend of Mills. His name had been brought to the attention of the Commission by Abner Graves, a mining engineer who lived in Denver, Colorado. In a letter to the Commission, Graves said he had gone to school with Doubleday at Coop-

Even if Abner Doubleday didn't invent baseball, the Union general did distinguish himself at the Battle of Gettysburg.

erstown. And he recalled seeing Doubleday organize a game called "Base Ball, for there were four bases in it . . ." Graves gave the year as 1839. And he implied that Doubleday had been disturbed by the fact that a ball game he and others were playing was badly organized and permitted too many players to compete. Doubleday, according to Graves, cut down the number of players and suggested the game be played between competing teams.

Although the Mills Commission seized on the letter as "evidence," most historians now reject it. They point out that Graves was more than 80 years old when he wrote the letter. He very likely would not have been able to recall accurately what had gone on so many years earlier. It was also noted that Doubleday could not have been in Cooperstown in 1839, for his military records show he was at West Point. In addition, Doubleday wrote several books and left a mountain of papers to his heirs. Nowhere did he mention baseball.

It now seems more likely that baseball evolved gradually into the game we know today. American boys and girls of the early 1800s were surely just as inventive as today's young players. Starting with the game of rounders or Base ball, they no doubt changed the official rules to suit the conditions under which the game was played. Thus there developed such games as one old cat and two old cat (using one and two bases). Then came town ball, with four bases and a batter's box between home base and first base.

All of these were variations on the

same principle. A ball was tossed to a batter. The batter hit the ball and ran to a base, or bases. The equipment and the methods of scoring and putting out runners or batters varied. One big difference between town ball and the other games was that the players were young men instead of children. In addition to whacking the ball with a bat, these older players took great delight in "soaking" or "stinging" base runners with the thrown ball.

Town ball—with its many variations—reached the height of its popularity in the early 1800s. It proved to be an excellent source of recreation in a world where automobiles, radios, and television sets were not even dreamed of. There was plenty of space in which to play, and equipment was cheap. Best of all, any red-blooded male could compete.

Soon the town-ball players began to form clubs. And the formation of the clubs represented the first step toward the game of professional baseball as we know it today.

2. The Gentlemen Players

For the most part, the first of the clubs organized solely for the purpose of playing "base ball" had as members young men who came from the wealthier branches of society. These high-born "gentlemen" played for exercise and a spot of fun. Most of them had played cricket, an English game that was very popular in America at the time. Though they found base ball more exciting, they still retained the genteel manners and sportsmanship of the cricket players.

The most famous ball-playing group of the early 1800s was the Knickerbocker Club of New York City. This organization enjoyed baseball immensely. The members met two or three times a week—first in Manhattan, then just across the Hudson River in New Jersey, where there was more room. The Knickerbockers soon realized that there was one great weakness to their favorite game—a lack of standard rules. To correct this fault, the officers of the club appointed a committee to draw up a set of rules and make copies for every member.

One of the committeemen was a six-foot, 200-pound player named Alexander Joy Cartwright, Jr. Cartwright, one of the club's best players, is generally given credit for getting the rules formulated and published. And because many of these rules include principles contained in today's regulations, Cartwright is often referred to as "The Father of Baseball."

The committee seems to have been the first to establish the baseball diamond by ruling that:

"The bases shall be from 'home' to second base, 42 paces, from first to third base, 42 paces, equidistant."

The principle of innings, with each team going to bat in turn, is embodied in the second Knickerbocker rule:

According to the rules of the New England Game, a base runner was out if hit by a thrown ball.

"The game shall consist of 21 counts or aces, but at the end *an equal number of hands* [innings] *must be played.*"

The third rule required that the ball "must be pitched, not thrown for the bat."

Other rules provided that a ball knocked outside the range of first or third base was foul. A player running the bases was out if the ball was in the hands of an opponent on the base, and the runner was touched by it before he reached the base. In no instance, however, was the ball to be thrown at him. When three players were out, all were out.

Players were to take their bat in regular turn. No base or ace—as they called a run—could be made on a foul strike. All disputes and differences related to the game were to be decided by the umpire, from whose decision there was no appeal.

The rules made two other points: they set the pitching distance at 45 feet and, apparently for the first time, limited each team to nine players.

Although baseball rules have undergone many, many changes through the years, they have always included better than half of the original Knickerbocker regulations, even if the wording has changed somewhat.

When the Cartwright committee, after many hours of intensive work, finally showed the first draft of the new rules to fellow club members, the Knickerbocker meeting place rang with shouted suggestions. Here was something new, something different, and something terribly exciting.

Finally the club president, Duncan F. Curry, quieted the members down. After a long, animated discussion, it was decided that the Knicks would invite a "nine" from the New York Club to play a match game at the Elysian Field in Hoboken, New Jersey, a short ferry ride from Manhattan. The game would be played under the newly written rules, and the loser would pay for a banquet at McCarty's Hotel, situated near the field. Alexander Cartwright was chosen to act as umpire.

The Knicks set the date for June 19, 1846, and the New York club promptly accepted the challenge. The first match game of record was on!

One of the early baseball games played at the Elysian Field in Hoboken, N. J.

The Knicks were so confident of victory they didn't bother to practice for the game. They were in for a surprise. The opposing pitcher—a well-known cricket bowler—whipped a little six-ounce ball with a rubber center past the Knick batters inning after inning. The Knicks got just one run. The New York team, meanwhile, scored 23 runs! Though the Knicks lost at their own game, the defeat was quickly forgotten at McCarty's Hotel, where a spirit of good fellowship and sportsmanship prevailed.

During the course of the game, Umpire Cartwright fined one of the players six cents "for cussin'." The club rules didn't permit such a thing, for baseball was a gentlemen's game. It wasn't to remain that way for long.

3. The Will to Win

The New York Nine either went back to cricket or disbanded, for the team never played the Knickerbockers again. As a matter of fact, the Knicks were unable to find another opponent for five years. Then suddenly, in the 1850s, organized clubs began to spring up everywhere—in New York, Philadelphia, Boston, Baltimore, Washington, D.C., and virtually every large eastern city. Although the Knicks had many requests for copies of their rules, some areas stubbornly held out against adopting them. As a result there developed the Philadelphia game, the Massachusetts game and, of course, the New York game, which was the Knickerbocker version.

As the years slipped by, the make-up of teams changed. The clubs were no longer limited to "gentlemen." Clerks, shopkeepers, accountants—almost any young man who could find the time— joined "the nines."

By the late 1850s well over 200 clubs had been organized. But there was constant bickering about the rules. In 1857 sixteen clubs formed the National Organization of Base Ball Players to establish a uniform playing code. One rule among those finally adopted was very important. It said members *could not accept money* for playing baseball.

The Civil War—which lasted from 1861 to 1865—hampered the activities of the National Organization, but it did much to popularize baseball. Union and Confederate soldiers played the game to keep fit and while away idle time. The game also found favor with prisoners of both armies. Sometimes the prisoners played against their captors.

Following the war, any young man worthy of his name had to sport a beard and play baseball. Teams formed at a faster rate than ever and heated rivalries began to grow between clubs representing different towns and communities.

Slowly the burning desire of teams to build a long string of victories spoiled the completely amateur status of the game. To get around the rule prohibiting direct payments, managers found jobs in factories or offices for the better players. The club members either didn't work at all at these jobs or at best worked only part time. The salaries they received were definitely for playing baseball.

One of the most famous of the post-Civil War teams—sometimes called "Muffin Nines"—was made up of players who worked for the federal government in Washington, D.C. This team, officially known as the Nationals, was probably the first to go on tour. A great crowd, cheering lustily and waving banners, saw the players off at Washington's Union Station.

They traveled a total of 2,400 miles by rail, boat, wagon, and horseback—a tremendous accomplishment for that day. In the space of about three weeks the Nationals played ten games, winning nine, some by such scores as 113–26, 106–21 and 88–12!

Their lone defeat came at the hands

of a club no one had heard much about. It was a team representing the little town of Rockford, Illinois. The pitcher for the Rockford nine—a tall, handsome, and powerful teen-ager named Albert Goodwill Spalding—had much to do with his team's victory. Spalding, to the amazement of all who saw or heard about the game, held the powerful Nationals to 23 runs, while the Rockford stalwarts scored 29.

The intense interest that people were showing in these games soon prompted newspapers and sporting magazines to report on the events. Some publications even assigned writers to travel with the principal teams when they were on tour. Naturally the reporting of games in the nation's newspapers and periodicals greatly heightened interest in baseball. As interest grew, so did the urge to win. These twin elements soon brought about a major change in baseball. It continued to be an amateur sport, but it also became a business. Its popularity was rapidly increasing.

4. The Brothers Wright

In the spring of 1866, Harry Wright, a muscular man of average build, left New York for Cincinnati. Wright was moving to the thriving Ohio city to take a job in a sports club as a cricket professional. Like the professional at today's golf clubs, Wright was to give lessons to members, arrange matches, and in general do what he could to stimulate interest in cricket.

Wright wasn't at the sports club very long before he discovered that the good citizens of Cincinnati were not much interested in cricket. Like hundreds of Americans in other cities, they had taken a liking to baseball.

This didn't pose too much of a problem for Wright. He knew as much about baseball as anyone. He and his brothers —Sam and George Wright—had played baseball as well as cricket. In no time at all, Harry Wright organized a ball team for the club. It was called the Red Stockings. Wright himself pitched, played center field, and managed the team.

He soon discovered a tough opponent in another Cincinnati nine, the Buckeyes. One season of play made him realize that the Red Stockings would need better players if they were to make a good showing against the Buckeyes and other strong teams. During the winter Wright contacted three players he knew in the East. He promised them good jobs in Cincinnati if they would join his Red Stockings. The trio accepted and, along with Wright, formed the heart of the Red Stocking team that took the field in 1868. It must have been a good team. The Buckeyes were beaten so badly and so often by the Red Stockings that they disbanded. But for the Red Stockings the 1868 season was only the beginning.

13

Wright's success with the three imported players set him to thinking. Why not bring in enough players to fill every position? And why not pay these players *directly* instead of pretending to place them in jobs? A salary for playing ball would have great appeal for players, Wright reasoned. It would also give the manager a better hold on them.

The more Wright thought about this idea the better he liked it, even though such a thing was unheard of at the time. Finally he made up his mind. He would write several good players and offer them a fair salary for joining the Red Stockings.

All through the off-season, Wright corresponded with ball players. One of them was his brother George, who had been playing with the Washington Nationals. By the spring of 1869, Wright had his team assembled. And when the Red Stockings took the field that year they became America's first professional baseball team.

It was a great team, too. In 65 games during that first season the Red Stockings were undefeated. Most of the games were played while the team was on a 12,000-mile tour, the longest taken by any ball team up to that time. By the season's end the Red Stockings had played before some 200,000 fans, another remarkable achievement.

The star of the team was undoubtedly George Wright, who received $1,400 for the season. Although not a large man, George had wonderful coördination. He was good at every sport. He was so skillful with bat and ball that he often put on juggling exhibitions before game time. It was George Wright who introduced the "pepper" game to baseball, a form of batting and fielding practice still in use.

George's play at his shortstop position brought plenty of "ooh's" and "aah's" from the fans. He was the first of the "roving" shortstops. While others played an almost stationary position to the right of the pitcher, George roamed the base line between second and third base. Crowds screamed with delight whenever he scampered in or out to snag the "bounding rock" and fire it to first base to retire a runner.

George was at his best during the famous Red Stocking tour. Playing in 52 games, he batted .518, scoring 339 times. Among his hits were 59 home runs.

Harry Wright guided the Red Stockings to another good season in 1870. By the middle of June, the team had stretched its winning streak to 80 games. The hard-fighting Atlantics of Brooklyn handed them their first defeat—8 to 7 in 11 innings before a record crowd of some 20,000.

The Red Stockings lost but five other games that year, two of them to the up-and-coming Chicago White Stockings.

But the Red Stockings—so skillfully put together and directed by Harry Wright—didn't last. Financial difficulties caused the club to disband. Soon Wright, his brother George, and a player named Gould moved to Boston, where they built another powerful team.

Harry Wright remained in baseball for many years and managed many winning teams. During these years he was constantly quoted in newspapers and

The championship Boston team organized by the Wright brothers in the 1870s. Al Spalding, pitcher, is standing second from left. George and Harry Wright are seated, third and fourth from left respectively.

magazines. The things he said had a profound effect on baseball.

Time and again, for example, he stressed the fact that if fans wanted to see good baseball they should pay a fair price for a ticket to watch a game. He thought the price should be fifty cents. Others argued that it ought to be half that amount.

Wright also believed that once in the ball park, the fan was entitled to see only the best efforts of the players. In an era when athletes lived recklessly and carelessly, Wright insisted on good behavior and physical conditioning. Throughout his lifetime he was admired and respected by all who came in contact with him. But, above all, he gave the game of baseball its first big push toward professionalism. And this is a contribution which should never be overlooked.

5. A Short, Unhappy Life

The astounding success of the Cincinnati Red Stockings in 1869 and 1870 made one thing all too clear to baseball promoters everywhere. To enjoy fame and, more important, to make money, a team must seek out the best players and pay them for their services.

Soon professional clubs began to join the National Association. But they had to fight hard to do so. The amateur members bitterly resented their intrusion. They saw many evils in the professional game. Gamblers followed the professional teams everywhere, betting openly in the stands. The players often joined in the betting. This led to corruption and dishonesty.

While the amateurs were still struggling to keep the professionals out of the National Association, a gambling scandal rocked the baseball world. It was proved that three members of the Mutuals had "thrown" a game to the Eckfords, a weaker team. The Eckfords won 28 to 11. A group of gamblers and Mutual players made a handsome profit on this dishonest bargain.

The amateurs had other complaints. They charged that the professionals flouted the rules in every way. They accused them of doing *anything* to win.

In addition, the professionals would leave one club and move to another at the slightest mention of more pay.

"Disgraceful!" the amateurs protested.

Obviously the two kinds of teams couldn't stay in the same organization. And they didn't. In the spring of 1871, representatives of ten professional teams met in New York. They formed the National Association of *Professional* Base Ball Players. The ten original members included:

The Philadelphia Athletics, Forest Cities of Rockford, Chicago White Stockings, Forest Cities of Cleveland, Boston Red Stockings, Troy Unions, New York Mutuals, Washington Olympics, Washington Nationals and the Kekiongas of Fort Wayne.

The formation of this second National Association was important for one very particular reason. The rules provided that member clubs were to play each other five times. The team winning the most games would then be considered baseball champions of the United States. This is how the first championship series was started.

The honor of winning the first pennant race went to Philadelphia. Harry Wright's Boston Red Stockings took the next four in a row.

The launching of the all-professional league and the establishment of a national championship looked wonderfully simple on paper. But these first professionals were sailing on a mighty leaky ship. Players who continually moved from one team to another caused the biggest problem. There was no legal way for the Association to make a player stay with his club. If the owner of the Athletics wanted to strengthen his team by hiring a pitcher working for the Boston Red Stockings, he simply approached the pitcher and offered him more money than he was already receiving.

Ball players didn't get much for their services. And since the playing season was short, they had a hard time indeed to earn enough to live on throughout the year. It was only natural that they should move to greener pastures whenever they could.

The owners had a money problem, too. They had to make a profit to survive. This meant they had to build a strong team and *win*. Fans have never gone to a ball park to watch a constant loser. As a result, the owners bid against each other for the better players.

By the time the Association was formed, many of the imperfections in the original Cartwright rules had been eliminated. There were still many loopholes, however, in the playing rules. The Association tried hard to correct them, for professional baseball had become a form of entertainment. To draw fans, the game had to be interesting, exciting.

The players found all sorts of ways to get around the rules. Little Dickey Pearce, a well-known shortstop in the

The Athletics play the Philadelphia Club in 1873. Note the umpire's top hat and the first baseman playing in foul ground.

1870s, harassed the opposition with a "fair-foul" hit. He would bunt the ball in such a way that it would land in fair territory, then roll into foul. Even the greenest amateur player knows that infielders have enough trouble handling a bunt that *stays* between the foul lines. To make a play on a bunt that lands in fair territory, then rolls way off into foul ground is impossible! Eventually the rulemakers were to make this particular play illegal.

Dishonesty, gambling, weak rules—all of these finally caused the collapse of America's first professional baseball organization. Another—the National League of Professional Base Ball Clubs —took its place.

6. Heroes and Heroics

Among the early players were names that will live forever. Some are known for a single feat; some became famous for years of wonderful performances; some made other contributions.

There was Al Spalding, for instance. When he pitched the Rockford nine to the stirring victory over the touring Washington team, Spalding was but 17 years old. It was a spectacular start. But it was only a start. Spalding carved an astounding career from the game he loved.

While pitching for Rockford, Spalding worked as a clerk in a grocery store at a small salary. But his strong right arm soon began to pay bigger dividends. After his first season at Rockford, he moved to Chicago to play. There he took another grocery-store job. The new position paid him $40 a week, many times his Rockford wage. The grocery failed, but Spalding returned to Rockford at the same pay.

Spalding did most of the pitching for Rockford. When the team played at home it won all but one game. This made the Rockford fans so excited they raised enough money to send the team on tour. They weren't disappointed either. For Spalding and the Rockford club again whipped the Washington Nationals. Then they defeated the openly professional Cincinnati Red Stockings.

By the time the next season rolled around, the Rockford fans decided to put an all-professional nine in the field. Spalding again joined the team. But soon Harry Wright wrote him from Boston, offering him a place on his new Red Stocking club. Spalding accepted and in his first year won 21 of 39 games. This was just the beginning. In his second year, he won 36 and lost 8. And during his last three years he won 149, averaging 49 a season! Spalding's best year was in 1875, when he won 56 and lost but five.

When Spalding and his Rockford teammates made their historic tour, one of their stops was at Marshalltown, a tiny hamlet in Iowa. The Marshalltown folk were as enthusiastic about baseball as fans in Rockford. And the nucleus of one of the very first Marshalltown teams was formed by three members of one family—the Ansons. Henry Anson, the oldest of the trio, was the father of the other two, Sturgis and Adrian.

The father played third base. Sturgis was at center field and Adrian at second base. Since Adrian was the youngest of the Ansons, he was usually referred to by fans and players as "Baby." But before he hung up his spikes and glove, Adrian was known by all baseball followers as "Pop." He was active in the big leagues for 27 years.

The Rockford promoters were so impressed with the Ansons that they offered the trio a chance to join the Rockford professional team the following season. Henry Anson declined, saying he and Sturgis had to stay in Marshalltown to tend the family business. But he gave young Adrian permission to leave home to play for Rockford.

Anson's first job as a professional ball player netted him $68 a month. But like Spalding he wasn't at Rockford long. At about the same time Spalding went to Boston, Adrian Anson joined the Philadelphia Athletics for a salary of $1,250 a year.

Anson, like Spalding, was a great player and an outstanding individual. He was courageous as a lion, fiercely honest, independent and stubborn. Anson was also opposed to drinking, gambling, and roistering. When playing ball he trained faithfully and watched his diet. On the diamond he played every game to the hilt. When he was manag-

Adrian "Cap" Anson brought fame to the Chicago White Stockings when he joined them in 1876.

ing he expected his players to play the same way.

Anson, Spalding, and the Wright brothers were but a few of the first professional players who made lasting contributions to the new game of baseball. In the 1860s Eddie Cuthbert startled the fans by sliding for a base. He did it by dropping on his seat and thrusting both

19

legs forward. Another player, Bob Addy, was even more daring. He slid head-first, riding on his stomach.

Pitchers soon learned how to make a baseball curve. They also threw a "dew drop." This was a pitch favored by Harry Wright whenever he left his usual outfield post for the pitcher's box. It was nothing more than a slow, looping delivery intended to upset the hitter's timing. Today it is called a "change of pace."

The king of the curve-ball pitchers was tiny Arthur "Candy" Cummings. His curve was so startling that fans refused to believe it. In one game, according to an old report, 24 of the batters he faced popped the ball into the air.

In addition to developing individual skills, the early professionals added something more to the game—aggressiveness. The game became faster, more exciting. Baseball was making great strides, but it was still only a beginning.

7. Birth of the National League

After the establishment of the National Association of Professional Base Ball Players in 1871, baseball became more than just a game. It developed into a business—a big business. As such, it attracted men who had money to invest. One of these investors was William A. Hulbert, a dynamic, forceful man. Hulbert put some of his money into owner-ship of the Chicago White Stockings in 1875. Soon he became an official of the club.

Hulbert quickly realized that baseball could not survive if the chaotic conditions that existed under the Professional Players Association continued. More-over, he felt the sport had to be run as a business. Along with a few friends, he set out to smash the Players Association and replace it with a stronger organiza-tion. Such a step called for strong action. And Hulbert was a strong man.

During the fall and winter of 1875–76, Hulbert maneuvered to build a new or-ganization to replace the tottering National Association. He called to New York representatives of clubs located in eight of the choicest cities in the nation —Chicago, St. Louis, Cincinnati and Louisville in the Midwest; New York, Philadelphia, Boston and Hartford in the East.

When all were assembled, Hulbert gave each man a copy of a new league constitution. He then argued the merits of five major proposals:

1. The new organization would be a league of *clubs*, not an association of players.
2. To become members, the clubs would pay an entry fee of $100, which was 10 times what it cost to join the Players Association.

3. Only clubs operating in cities with a population of 75,000 or more would be eligible. League clubs would also have to stay at least five miles away from other clubs.

4. Players' contracts were to be written, not verbal. If a player was considered ineligible for one club, he would be ineligible for all.

5. Any player found guilty of being dishonest on the diamond was to be barred by the League for life.

While these proposals seem very simple and logical, Hulbert did not have an easy time persuading the club representatives to accept them. He cajoled, threatened, and argued from early morning until late at night. Finally the club representatives gave in to Hulbert's persuasiveness. They voted to adopt "Hulbert's Reform," as the five points came to be known. Later developments were to prove that this was one of the biggest events in baseball history.

With Morgan Bulkeley as League president, the eight clubs played a 70-game schedule. Each team played every other team five games at home and five away. All was not smooth sailing, however, during the National League's first year. Chicago was delighted with the performance of the White Stockings, but fans in other cities lost interest in the flag race. The playing rules also continued to be a problem. The players still found ways to get around them. The power balance between pitcher and batter had not been struck, either. If the rules favored the pitcher, there were few hits and few runs. If they favored the batter, there were too many runs.

Faced with losses at the gate and a growing dissatisfaction among the fans, the club owners elected Hulbert as League president for the 1877 season. They hoped he could straighten things out.

Hulbert went right to work. He first expelled New York and Philadelphia because they had not played the full 70 games on their schedules. Thus the League started the season with six teams. It finished with even fewer. Cincinnati failed to pay its dues, so Hulbert cancelled all Cincinnati games.

In addition to his other troubles, the newspapers publicly criticized Hulbert for his dual role as president of the National League and official of the White Stockings. Many thought he was more interested in the success of the Chicago ball club than in the affairs of the League. But despite everything, the League stuck together and continued to play baseball.

8. A New Ingredient: Color

While the club owners and National League officials struggled to establish a profitable and smooth-running business, an important change was taking place on the diamond. The ball player was beginning to emerge as a national personality.

Al Spalding, of course, had been one of the first to win fame. But after his first season with the White Stockings, Spalding retired from active play. Into his place as playing manager stepped Adrian Anson.

Anson brought fame to Chicago. In his first six years as pilot of the White Stockings, the team won four pennants and never finished lower than fourth. Anson was the team's best hitter. In 20 of the 22 years he played, Anson batted .300 or better. (To bat .300 a player must average three hits out of every ten times at bat.) He ended with a lifetime average of .339, twice hitting over .400 (.407 in 1879 and .421 in 1887). Anson is one of the few players in the entire history of the game who banged out more than 3,000 hits.

Anson taught his players many new things. One of these was to shorten the grip on the bat (choke up) and hit the ball to unprotected areas (place-hit).

Along with Anson's powerful bat, the Chicago club had fine pitchers in Fred Goldsmith and Lawrence Corcoran.

And behind the plate the White Stockings had a catcher who, perhaps more than any other player of his day, electrified the fans whenever he put his foot on the diamond. He was Michael J. Kelly, whose skill at batting, running, and throwing earned him the title of "King of the Diamond." It was Kelly who discovered how to throw his flying body to one side and reach out and touch the base with the tip of a pointed toe. Kelly taught his method of sliding to his teammates and it quickly become known as "the Chicago slide." Today it is called the "hook slide," or "fadeaway."

Kelly enjoyed great popularity at Chicago. But in the biggest player deal of baseball's first decade, he was sold to Boston for $10,000. It was an unheard-of price, but Boston quickly got its money back. The Beantown fans idolized their "$10,000 Beauty," as Kelly was called. Whenever he got on base, a tremor of excitement ran through the Boston rooters. They would chant in unison: "Slide, Kelly! Slide!" Kelly rarely disappointed.

For a long time the same nine players who started a game had to finish it. But finally the League put in a substitution rule. The rule, however, proved to have a weakness, and Kelly was the one who pointed it out. During a game he was sitting on the bench while his team was on the field. A rival batter hit a pop-up that was out of reach of the regular Boston catcher. Instead, the ball came straight toward Kelly.

"Kelly now catching!" the King roared as he sprang from the bench and snared the ball. Kelly argued that the batter was out. "It's right there in the rules," he cried. "It says a substitute may enter the game *at any time*."

Kelly didn't win that argument, but the substitution rule was changed to read that a new player may enter the game only when the ball is dead (not in play). This rule still applies.

Another early star who had the appeal of Kelly and Anson was little Arlie Latham. In addition to being a skillful ball player, Latham was an expert tumbler with a delightful sense of humor. Once, as he charged to first base to beat out an

Dashing Mike Kelly in the days when he was running the Allentown, Pa., Baseball Club.

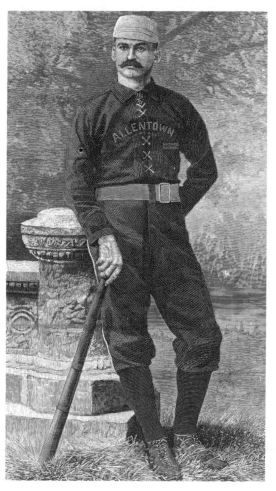

infield roller, he looked up to see Cap Anson crouching in the base line, ball in hand. Instead of slowing, or dodging, Latham kept right on. Just when a crash seemed inevitable, he took a dive right over Anson's head and landed hands-first in back of the startled first baseman. Turning a neat forward roll, he continued on.

Still another player who made a name for himself was Hugh Daily. He was a pitcher with but one arm. Daily had lost his left arm when a boy. He was burned severely in a theater fire and the arm had to be amputated. By the time he reached early manhood, however, he had thrown a baseball past some of the most feared hitters in the nation—Kelly, Anson, and George Wright.

Daily's name first appeared in headlines in 1880, when he pitched the New York Metropolitans to a 4 to 2 victory over Washington. In addition to pitching well, he knocked in the winning run with a single. During his second season with the Metropolitans, an independent team, Daily won 38 games. This was quite a record, considering the fact that he was unable to play during the month of June.

Daily, who also played the infield and outfield, eventually pitched in the National League. In 1883 he hurled a no-hit, no-run game against Philadelphia.

All of these players—Kelly, Anson, Latham, Daily, and too many more to mention—brought to baseball that indefinable quality called "color." Fans have been looking for it in ball players ever since. Luckily they always seem to find it.

9. Baseball's First War

To stay alive through the 1870s, the National League was forced to fight a dogged, running battle on two fronts. The fracas started because William Hulbert, Harry Wright, and a few others tried to limit League membership to eight clubs and hold down player salaries. The salaries were the club owner's biggest item of expense.

Although the independent ball clubs were fairly successful—especially those with a player like Daily in the lineup—they wanted to be put on the same footing as National League teams. They also wanted to participate in the race for the "championship." It would help fill their pockets with money.

But the National League officials, on one pretense, then another, refused to admit the independents to membership.

"They've got a monopoly!" the independents cried.

To which the National Leaguers replied with a shrug, "This is the only way we can run a sound, profitable business."

While the National League owners grimly held off the independents, they struggled to control their own players and player salaries. Unfortunately a player could sell his services to any team once the season ended. Hulbert himself had lured players away from other teams, but he was among the first to recognize the danger of such a practice.

"If we constantly bid against each other for players, salaries will eventually go so high we'll all be ruined," he warned.

Hulbert had also introduced a regulation which stated that a player ineligible for one team was ineligible for all. Thus, if a player disobeyed a club's rules, he could be put on a black list. No other League team owner would hire him.

Even this wasn't enough to satisfy the owners. Hulbert and his colleagues introduced the most controversial rule baseball has ever known—the "reserve" clause.

The principle was simple: At the end of the season, each team put all of its players on a reserve list. The owners were pledged not to hire, or attempt to hire, a player on the reserve list of another team, unless the player was released.

In other words, if a player was dissatisfied with his employer, he was no longer free to move to another team. He was the property of the team to which he was under contract.

The National League's attitude angered scores of independent club owners, players, and the public. Something was bound to happen, and in the winter of 1881 it did. Alfred H. Spink, a sports writer, led a drive to form a new major league called the American Association. Charter members included the Atlantics of Brooklyn, the Alleghenys of Pittsburgh, the Athletics of Philadelphia, the Cincinnati Reds, the St. Louis Browns and the Eclipse Club of Louisville. (The Atlantics dropped out before the start of the 1882 season, and were replaced by Baltimore.)

Baseball and its questionable pleasures—as pictured in an 1883 newspaper.

What is it? — Suspected to be the Umpire

Look Out

A Drawn Game

Just in time

Shoot the

The American Association adopted many National League rules, but it differed in three important ways. The clubs played on Sundays and holidays. The sale of beer was permitted in the ball parks, and admission was 25 cents, only half as much as the National League price.

The National League had nothing but contempt for the American Association. It sneered openly at every move made by the new league.

Soon the two leagues opened an all-out battle for talent. The American Association, with the backing of wealthy beer brewers, caused scores of good players to break their National League contracts. The National League owners quickly raised their salaries and lured players back. Some of the cases of contract-breaking landed in court, with one league suing the other.

In spite of the bickering, the American Association flourished. Fans liked Sunday ball, the low admission price, and the serving of beer at the ball parks. They also saw good baseball.

The Cincinnati Reds won the first pennant in the new league in 1882 and promptly arranged a series of games with the championship White Stockings of the National League. This might have turned into the first "World Series," but after each team won one game, the remainder of the games were called off. Angry league officials were opposed to any mingling of American Association and National League teams.

Then William Hulbert died unexpectedly, and A. H. Soden finished his term as National League president. The next year Colonel A. G. Mills, a man of great skill and patience, became president. Mills saw that the raiding between the two leagues could not go on. So he maneuvered leaders of both groups to a peace meeting, along with representatives of the Northwestern League, a minor circuit.

By the time the meeting was over, all three organizations had reached agreement on how future baseball business would be conducted. Essentially, the three leagues vowed to respect each other's territorial and player rights and, especially, the reserve list.

For a few years all went well. Baseball prospered. An attempt to start another major league in 1884 ended in failure. But the National League and the American Association continued to thrive. Realizing that they had to work together, they worked out a rule to control the sale of players from teams of one league to teams in the other. For example, if an American Association team wanted to sell a player to a National League team, it could do so only if all other teams in the Association approved. This is now known as the "waiver" rule.

Changes on the diamond helped baseball, too. Most of the changes concerned the rules that applied to pitcher and batter. The number of bad pitches that sent a batter to first base was gradually reduced from nine to four. The pitcher was also permitted, for the first time, to throw with any motion. The batter, however, still had the right to call for a high, or low, pitch.

10. Charles Comiskey

One new development above all others gave baseball a big boost. That was the practice of arranging games between league winners after the close of the season. Started by the Providence Grays and the New York Metropolitans in 1884, the post-season games met with immediate success.

A great new name—Charles A. Comiskey—was linked to the next four championship games. Comiskey, the Chicago-born son of a hard-working builder, was exposed to baseball at an early age. As a boy, he constantly irritated his father because of his interest in the game.

"Baseball is just a lot of tomfoolery," his father would complain. "To make a living, a man has to work, not play a game!"

Although Charles had great respect for his father, he couldn't overcome the lure of the diamond. He played with any amateur team that would take him. When his father sent him to college, he played on the college nine.

Soon after college, young Comiskey signed a contract with the Dubuque (Iowa) Rabbits for a small salary. Not long afterward, the tall, lean youngster won a first-base job with the St. Louis Browns. Then he became playing manager of the Browns.

Young Comiskey was both intelligent and hard-working. As manager of the Browns, he brought much to baseball. He introduced a big change in the way the infielders worked together on defense. First basemen, for instance, had always played close enough to the base to touch it. This meant that the second baseman had to try to field almost every ground ball batted between first and second.

Comiskey dropped the first-base position back and away from the base. In this way, the distance between first and second was covered by two players instead of one. As part of this change, Comiskey also taught his pitchers to run and cover first base whenever the first baseman fielded a grounder and could not make the put-out alone.

Comiskey tightened team defense even more by having infielders back up throws to the bases. If an outfield throw got past the third baseman, for example, another player was there to stop it and keep the runner from advancing.

This kind of baseball was apparently quite effective. The Browns, under Comiskey, won four pennants in a row, starting in 1885. Their first post-season opponent was the Chicago White Stockings with Adrian Anson as manager. The Chicago club was every bit as powerful as the Browns. The two teams met in both the second and third championship series. And what titanic struggles they were! The first time the teams played each other, the Browns won three, tied one, and lost three—one on a forfeit. The forfeit came about in the second game, when Comiskey took his team off the field after an umpire made a call he didn't like. The Browns claimed that the forfeited game didn't count and

27

that they were the winners of the series.

The next year the Browns defeated the White Stockings in a six-game series. In 1887, however, they lost to Detroit in a fifteen-game match. The following season, 1888, they lost to New York in a ten-game series.

With the improvement in diamond play and league relationships, interest in baseball was at an all-time high. But unfortunately the owners and players were not getting along with each other.

11. The Battle Lines Are Drawn

The black list, the reserve list, and the new agreement among the professional leagues gave the baseball owners and officials tremendous power over the players.

The first abuse of this power occurred in 1885, when the leagues voted to limit players' salaries to $2,000. The clubs were also forbidden to give the players any advance salary during the winter. This worked a great hardship on players whenever they were faced with an emergency at home, or when they needed money to travel to meet the team at the start of the season.

The owners made matters worse by imposing fines and suspensions (without pay) for minor violations of the rules. One owner went so far as to fine a player for not tipping his hat when they passed on the street. Such treatment made the players bitter and angry. They talked of joining together to fight the owners.

The first move in that direction took place in the fall of 1885. The New York Giants formed a chapter of a new organization called The Brotherhood of Professional Base Ball Players. President of the organization was handsome, popular John Montgomery Ward, the Giants' pitcher and shortstop. Once the New York players were organized, Ward began to form chapters among other clubs. As the Brotherhood grew, the players began to make known their position on various issues. They asked that full salaries be written into their contracts. And they demanded that an end be put both to the rule limiting salaries and to the hated reserve list. By the end of the 1887 season, the Brotherhood had almost 100 members enrolled. They felt it was time to discuss matters with the owners and demand recognition for themselves.

At Al Spalding's suggestion, the National League agreed to talk with the Brotherhood representatives. The owners, however, played a shrewd game. They were very polite and agreed to a few minor changes in player rules. Then they pointed out that, after all, the players were already signed for the following year. Furthermore, the American Association was not represented.

How could they make any further changes?

John Ward may have seen through these tactics, but he probably felt the Brotherhood was not strong enough to risk an open fight. In any event, he agreed it would be useless to press matters further.

The playing season of 1888 followed its usual course. And after it ended, the hard-fisted owners forgot many of their previous promises to the Brotherhood.

At first this deceit didn't seem to matter. Most of the players were excited about something else. They had heard that Al Spalding was taking two teams to New Zealand and Australia. The prospect of a long ocean voyage to strange lands struck the fancy of American baseball players and fans. In fact it seemed almost unbelievable at a time when a trip across one's home state was a rarity.

The talk about the trip turned out to be true. Spalding, one of the owners of the Chicago White Stockings and president of a sporting-goods firm, had succeeded in arranging such a tour.

One of the two teams to make the trip was the White Stockings, managed by Cap Anson. The other was the All-Americans, a group of what would now be called "all-stars." The All-Americans were picked by their manager, John Ward.

The tour was significant in many ways. The President of the United States gave the team a send-off at a White House reception. This was a new and high honor for baseball. Later, amidst much excitement, the party of 35 players and their wives started their long westward journey from Chicago. On the way to the Pacific Coast, the teams

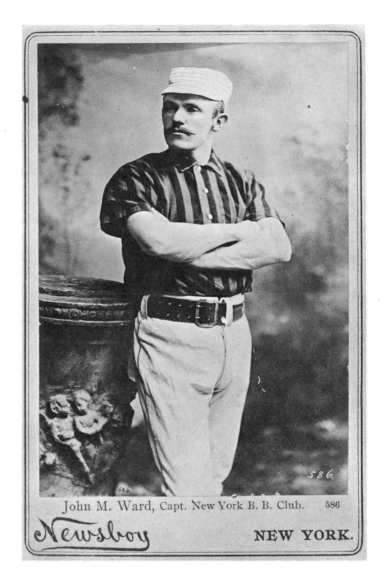

John M. Ward, Capt. New York B. B. Club.   586

Newsboy   NEW YORK.

played in Denver, Omaha, and other cities. Few people west of Chicago had ever seen big-league baseball. Wherever the teams played, they were watched by great crowds of people, many of whom had traveled miles.

In Sydney, Australia, the All-Americans and the White Stockings played before 5,500 spectators. In Melbourne the crowd numbered 11,000. By the time the Australian trip was finished, the players had been invited to extend their tour to Africa, Asia, and Europe. They went next to Ceylon, then to Egypt, where they actually played a ball game on the desert sands near the ancient pyramids.

From Egypt the Americans traveled to Rome, where games were played on royal grounds before the King of Italy and his court. Leaving Rome, the group went on to Florence, then northward to France and England.

While John Ward, the president of the Brotherhood, was off on this expedition, the team owners were busily fashioning a new noose to slip around the necks of their ball players. Originated by John T. Brush, owner of the Indianapolis team, it was called the Classification Plan. Under the plan, the best players were classified as "A" players. They were to receive $2,500 a year and no more. The next best player was put in the "B" classification and was to receive $2,250. The new pay scale went all the way down to $1,500 for Class "E" players.

The owners claimed to have rated each player on conduct and effort. The plan shocked the players, but the owners said they would be blackballed if they didn't agree to the plan. With Ward away and no one else willing to lead the Brotherhood, the situation seemed hopeless to the players. Most of them reluctantly signed contracts. Thus the owners succeeded in putting the Classification Plan into effect. They were soon to regret it.

12. The Revolt

The steamer *Adriatic*, bearing the touring American baseball teams, was sighted off Long Island on April 6, 1889. She was three days late. Her tardiness, however, had not discouraged those awaiting her arrival. Some had important news to convey to John Ward. Others were anxious to speak with Al Spalding.

Two boats were already racing to meet the *Adriatic* in the farther reaches of Lower New York Bay. One was the steamer *Laura M. Storin*, "loaded with lovers of baseball," as one newspaper put it. The other was a tugboat, carrying a score of prominent actors and actresses, presumably lovers of the game.

When the three vessels came together, a great cheer went up amid a shriek of foghorns and whistles and the clanging of ship's bells.

In Egypt, Spalding's American baseball party posed under the broken nose of the Sphinx.

Very quickly a gangplank was run out to bridge the gap between the *Adriatic* and the *Laura M. Storin*. The ball players and their wives piled aboard the little steamer, which quickly made her way back to the island of Manhattan.

Not until the party was on its way to breakfast at the Fifth Avenue Hotel did John Ward learn how the Brotherhood had been betrayed by the new Classification Plan. When he tried to protest to Al Spalding a few days later, Ward was told there was nothing to discuss.

Spalding's blunt dismissal was too much even for patient John Ward. That summer the players began to meet secretly. Their plan? A new league. A committee was formed to raise funds. They had no difficulty, for Ward and his friends knew a number of men with money to invest who were sympathetic to baseball. As soon as these men were approached, however, word of the Brotherhood plans leaked out.

Spalding was one of the first to hear. He tried to arrange a meeting with Ward. But Ward said simply:

"Remember, Al, there's nothing to discuss."

By the fall of 1889, the players and their new owners formed a partnership to operate the "Players' League." John Ward called the press to a downtown Manhattan hotel early in November to make the official announcement. Along with the plans for the new league, Ward issued a blistering "manifesto."

"... There was a time," it went, "when the League stood for integrity and fair dealing. Today it stands for dollars and cents. Once it looked to the elevation of the game and an honest exhibition of the sport. Today its eyes are upon the turnstiles. Men have come into the business for no other motive than to exploit it for every dollar in sight. Measures originally intended for the good of the game have been turned into instruments for wrong. . . . Players have been bought and sold and exchanged as though they were sheep instead of American citizens. . . ."

The launching of the Players' League in 1890 started another all-out baseball war. With rules that abolished the abuses and included profit-sharing, the League drew almost every big-name player in the major leagues. About the only big star of the day who did not join was stubborn Cap Anson.

The American Association and the National League, united and experienced, fought the Players' League in every way imaginable. They scheduled games wherever and whenever the Players' games were scheduled. They pooled their money to carry the weaker teams. They changed their contracts and offered bonuses and bigger contracts to members of the Players' League if they would leave the new league.

In a typical attempt to break the Brotherhood, Spalding had a secret meeting with Michael Kelly who, at that time, was at the peak of his ability.

After a preliminary discussion, Spalding laid a check in front of Kelly.

"As you will notice, that check is good for $10,000 and payable to you," Spalding said to the king. "That's yours for signing with our league. On top of that, you can have a three-year contract."

"For how much?" Kelly countered.

"You can fill in the amount of salary yourself."

Kelly looked Spalding squarely in the eye. Convinced that Spalding meant what he said, Kelly replied:

"I'll take a walk and think it over. Meet you here in half an hour."

Kelly's walk lasted about two hours.

"Al," he said on his return, "I just can't do it. I can't go back on the Brotherhood—all my friends."

Kelly paused for a moment, then added: "And neither would you, Al."

"I understand," Spalding said. "And you're right—I wouldn't either."

The fans, however, became discouraged and disgusted with all the scrapping. Because their favorite players were continually moving from one team to another, they found it hard to get into a rooting frame of mind. Then too it was hard to decide which game to attend if two or three teams were playing in the same city on the same day. As a result the fans stayed away from the ball parks. And all three leagues lost a tremendous amount of money.

At first it was hard to tell just who was winning the battle. All the teams gave out false attendance figures. Then came one seemingly sure indication. Cincinnati of the American Association, unable to keep afloat financially, sold out to the Players'. This was a bitter blow to the opponents of the Players' League. By the end of the season, almost everybody seemed to be in the mood for a compromise. Even the backers of the Players' League—as distinct from the Brotherhood—were looking for a way out of the unhappy war.

There were many secret meetings, and out of these grew three committees—one representing each league. Al Spalding was head of the National League committee. Smart as a fox when it came to business, Spalding found a way to break the Players' League. He did it by insisting that he could meet only with the financial backers of the Players' League. Ward and the other members of the Brotherhood, he said, did not have control of the money, so how could they speak for the owners?

Ward fought hard to maintain a united stand. But he could not overcome Spalding's "divide and conquer" methods. One by one, the backers of the Players' League teams sold out.

By winter there was no more Players' League. In its place was a new line-up of major league teams, covered by a new set of rules.

With the Players' League dead and a costly war ended, all should have been peaceful and serene in the world of baseball. But it wasn't; there were other arguments. Before the 1891 season opened, baseball was in its fourth war in 15 years! The pattern was the same as in all the war years. Rival leagues were plotting against each other for players.

By the end of 1891, the major leagues were again looking for peace. And they had the usual reason—losses at the gate.

To end all their troubles, they agreed to a grand new plan. The strongest teams in both leagues would be merged into one—The National League and the American Association of Professional

Base Ball Clubs. (Actually only four Association teams—Baltimore, Washington, St. Louis, and Louisville—joined the eight existing National League teams to form the big new organization.)

With one unified 12-team league, it seemed as if there would be little opportunity for any more fighting.

13. From Infancy to Adolescence

With the start of the first 12-team major league, a change came over baseball. New and younger players began to appear. The playing rules came closer to perfection. And the term "inside baseball" came into use.

Harry Wright had introduced the first noticeable team play. Spalding, Anson, then Comiskey, helped develop it. But Frank Selee, the manager of the Boston National League team, was the one who made so much of it that the fans took notice. Selee, for example, favored the hit-and-run play, which has thrilled fans for years. Selee's method was a little different from the one in use today, but the principle is the same.

When you look at a baseball team in the field, you will notice that the first and second basemen space themselves so they can cover most of the area between first and second base. The third baseman and shortstop share the area between second and third. If any of these players pull out of position, a large hole is left in the defense.

Frank Selee found a way to *make* the defensive players move. When he had a runner on first, he would signal for the hit-and-run play. As the pitcher got ready to throw to the batter, the runner on first base would break for second. Either the shortstop or second baseman, or both, would have to rush to cover second. They had to guard against a steal of second. The batter, of course, would then try to knock the ball through the hole in the defense. If he was successful, the runner could get one or two extra bases. An extra base was very important in the era of the dead ball.

Selee's teams won three pennants in a row, starting in 1891. The Boston fans were delighted with the power and speed of Selee's team. But interest in the remaining 11 cities lagged. It was obvious that the fans preferred the excitement of two pennant races in smaller and better balanced leagues. They liked the after-season climax, too. This was missing in the 12-team circuit.

In an attempt to spark more interest, the league went to a "split season" in 1892. They established for the first time a 154-game schedule and decided that the winner of the first half would play the winner of the second half for the championship.

Boston won the top spot in its half of the league. And a new name among ball players led Cleveland to victory in the other half of the league. The team was the Cleveland Spiders. The new player —Denton True Young.

Young was an industrious farm boy who stood six feet two in his spikes and tipped the scale at 210 pounds. An ability to throw a tremendous fast ball gave Young a nickname that made fans forget his first and second names. As he was warming up one day in front of an old wooden backstop, his catcher let two or three pitches go by. Each time that happened, the ball whizzed into the backstop, breaking a board.

"Boy, looks like a cyclone hit it," commented Young's manager as he inspected the damage. From then on, the rawboned youngster was known as "Cyclone," or "Cy" Young.

Young made an auspicious start when he broke into baseball. He struck out Cap Anson the first time he faced the fearsome Chicago hitter. Young also ended his career spectacularly. In 22 seasons, he amassed 510 victories, a record number of games too—906.

When Boston and Cleveland met in the first game of their play-off series, the game ended in an 11-inning scoreless tie that was called off because of darkness. Boston won the remaining games, however.

While 1893 was the year Boston won its third straight pennant, it was also the year the pitching rules underwent their last major change. The pitching distance went to 60 feet 6 inches, which is what it is today at almost all levels of baseball played by those 13 and older.

Other rules, too, had become more

Because of the way he pitched, Denton True Young earned the nickname of "Cy"—short for cyclone.

stabilized. The number of bad pitches that entitled a batter to a base had gradually changed from nine, to eight, to seven, to five, and finally, to four. At the start of the 1883 season, the pitcher was permitted to throw the ball from any spot beneath his shoulder. But all restrictions were lifted the next year.

For a long time the batter had been able to tell the pitcher where he wanted the ball thrown. If the pitcher failed to comply, the batter was awarded first base. On the other hand, the umpire couldn't call a strike unless the pitch was in a zone indicated by the batter. By 1888, this was eliminated and the traditional "three strikes and out!" call was started.

With that change, baseball moved into one of its most exciting eras.

14. The Original Orioles

Under Ned Hanlon, the Baltimore Orioles of 1894 became the greatest team in baseball. They were greater even than the past teams of the Cincinnati Red Stockings, Chicago White Stockings, and the Boston machines built by Frank Selee.

The Orioles boasted only one star, Wee Willie Keeler. But they didn't need to be great individually, for they played as no other nine had done up to that time. They played as a *team*.

One of the Oriole players of that day was a scrawny, runty third baseman with oversized ears. His name was John McGraw. He didn't look big enough to make the average high school team. But what he lacked in size, McGraw made up for in skill, courage, and sheer ferocity.

A native of upstate New York, McGraw was the son of poor parents. His love for baseball drove his father to dis-

traction. He lived and breathed the game from the day he was strong enough to pick up a bat and ball to the day he died.

Townspeople shook their heads in wonder as they watched McGraw grow up. He practiced throwing and hitting at every opportunity. When he became old enough to work, he worked only to earn money for buying baseball equipment. He was especially fond of rule books, buying every new one published.

McGraw first played professional baseball in the New York-Pennsylvania League in 1890. He was still a youngster. The following year he joined several other players and signed to play for a Florida team for "board, shaving and washing expenses and a cigar a week." His smart heads-up play, deft glove, accurate throwing arm, and consistent batting soon got him into the majors.

Another talented Oriole player was

catcher Wilbert Robinson. A good-natured hulk of a man, Robinson was easily one of the smartest players in baseball.

The Orioles were a brash, swashbuckling crew who liked, above all else, to win ball games. And by any means. Some of their efforts were scientific; some were a clear evasion of the rules. As an example of the former, the Orioles used the hit-and-run play to perfection. Against the Giants in the opening game in 1894, for example, they used it 13 times successfully. They also developed something new: the "squeeze" play. Just as today, a runner on third base broke for the plate as the pitcher delivered the ball. The batter bunted the ball, enabling the runner to score.

As an example of their not-so-scientific methods, the Oriole outfield often planted extra baseballs in the high outfield grass before play started. If a sharp liner bounded by the outfielders, the nearest player didn't have to chase the ball until it stopped rolling. All the outfielder had to do was pick up one of the planted balls and hurl it into play.

This plan backfired one day as two outfielders ran after a ball driven between them. One Oriole picked up a hidden ball, whirled, and threw to the infield. At the same time the other Oriole tossed in the batted ball. The umpire was quick to catch on. He forfeited the game to the Orioles' opponent!

McGraw and his mates not only used the hidden-ball trick, they also blocked the base paths and held on to runners whenever they could do so without get-

John McGraw, the runty Oriole third baseman with oversized ears.

ting caught. One of McGraw's favorite tricks was to grab a runner by the belt when he tried to break for the plate after the catch of a fly ball by the outfield. This, too, went amiss one day. His opponent knew the trick and unbuckled his belt when McGraw wasn't looking. The fly ball plopped into an Oriole outfielder's glove and the runner lit out for home. McGraw, dumbfounded, was left with a belt dangling from his hand.

In 1894 the Orioles swept to their very first pennant. And they repeated their success the next two years. The original Orioles left an unmistakable mark on baseball. And through the many Oriole players who later became managers—McGraw, Robinson, and Hugh Jennings —the spirit of that famous team was carried to others.

15. Fandom Balks

In spite of the many improvements in baseball during the 1890s, the conduct of the game dipped to a new low. The owners were foolish in the way they ran their top-heavy league. Though they had the monopoly they had always wanted, they were so greedy and selfish they almost wrecked their business.

To begin with, the owners were dishonest with each other. For example, it was the practice for visiting teams and home teams to share the gate proceeds on a percentage basis (usually 60% for the home team, 40% for the visitors). In a number of instances, the home team falsely reported gate receipts. This meant the visiting team failed to get its fair share.

The deals involving sales and trades of players were often crooked, too. The owners were as ruthless with the players as they had been before the Brotherhood revolt. When the National League and the American Association merged, it was agreed that all players who signed contracts before December, 1891, were to go back to the clubs holding these contracts. All other players' names were thrown into a pool. From this pool the teams picked enough men to fill a 15-man roster. The leftover players were sent to the minor leagues.

The following year, to hold down expenses, the owners cut two men from each team. They then arbitrarily reduced salaries—some by as much as 40%! The owners abused their rigid control over the players in other ways. They fined them at the slightest whim, held back salaries, and refused to pay legitimate expenses.

The owners apparently didn't care about the interests and loyalties of the fans either. Many invested in more than one team. This made the fans wonder if teams were competing on a fair basis. John T. Brush, for example, owned stock in both Cincinnati and the New York

Giants. And in 1899 the owner of the Cleveland Spiders also owned the St. Louis entry. Because St. Louis seemed a more profitable location than Cleveland, this owner moved his best players to St. Louis. To the disgust and indignation of the Cleveland fans, the Spiders finished with the worst record in baseball. They lost 134 games and won but 20!

On top of all this, the owners paid little attention to what was going on between the foul lines. The diamond often appeared to be more of a place for a gang fight than for a ball game. Because the players were out to win by fair means or foul—and more often foul than fair—brawling and fighting became common. The umpires had no authority.

The League paid them a small sum to run ball games, then forgot about them.

For a while one umpire handled the games. A two-umpire system was started in 1895, but matters didn't improve. The poor umpires were stomped on, pushed, and generally abused. The owners were too busy listening to the click of the turnstiles to take notice.

As baseball moved through the 1890s, some of its worst features came to the fore. Competition was tainted, and teams were often out of control. And the owners, in their greediness, ignored the public. This short-sighted handling of America's newest and biggest entertainment business was to have unfortunate results which the owners would soon regret.

16. A New League, a New Attitude

There was unrest in many quarters over the policies of the National League, especially when the League slowly began to fall apart.

One of those who had new ideas about baseball was Charles Comiskey. While managing the Cincinnati Reds, Comiskey met a big, dynamic sports writer for the Cincinnati *Commercial-Gazette*. His name was Bancroft Johnson. Soon they became fast friends. Like all good friends they had a common interest. Theirs was baseball, but not the kind of baseball then in style. Comiskey and Johnson wanted clean baseball—baseball for the fans.

In 1894, at Comiskey's suggestion, a number of teams formed a minor league in the north-central area of the country. Called the Western League, it included such cities as Minneapolis, Milwaukee, Toledo, Kansas City, Detroit, Sioux City, Grand Rapids, and Indianapolis. Comiskey attended the first meeting of the new organization and agreed to take the franchise at St. Paul. He nominated Ban Johnson for president of the League, and Johnson was promptly accepted.

During this fateful meeting, the Milwaukee franchise was given to a man

Cornelius McGillicuddy, better known to baseball fans as Connie Mack.

Charles A. Comiskey

named Cornelius McGillicuddy, a tall, skinny ex-catcher who became known to later generations as Connie Mack. Mack, like Comiskey, had played and managed in the Players' League. Mack was happy to be in the Western League. Like Comiskey and Johnson, he was opposed to drinking, gambling, and rowdyism.

As a young catcher, Mack had been one of the first to try to distract opposing hitters by chattering away at them as they stood at the plate. But he was always polite. Once he even apologized for tipping an opponent's bat.

As Mack, Comiskey, and Johnson worked to build up the Western League, they looked ahead to the time when they could bring it into competition with the National League. The baseball monopoly that existed in the 1890s was very strong, however. Those who wished to oppose it—and there were many—had to move carefully.

In 1899 Ban Johnson announced that the Western Association was reorganizing and would take the field in 1900 as the American League.

While this was going on, the National League was having internal trouble. As the teams lost money, the owners drifted into two warring camps. One side backed Andrew Freedman, an owner of the New York Giants. The other side opposed him.

As one way of getting out of their difficulties, the National League dropped four teams for 1900. Ban Johnson quickly moved an American franchise into one of the cities, Cleveland. He also put Comiskey in Chicago with another American League franchise. These two moves angered the National League, even though Johnson clearly indicated he was not interested in starting another baseball war.

With the launching of the American League, Johnson put a new face on baseball. His methods were simple. He took a strong stand with the players. He appointed a good corps of umpires, treated them fairly, and backed their every decision. The American League games were run in an orderly manner. Rowdyism, drinking, gambling, and profanity were prohibited. Those who didn't abide by Johnson's rules were fined and suspended.

The fans were weary of the type of baseball being played in the National League. They were also suspicious of the shadowy operations of the owners. Right from the start, they supported the infant American League, enabling it to become a fairly prosperous organization.

By the end of that first year, however, the American League had learned that it was useless to try to exist peacefully with the haughty National Leaguers.

"If they want a war, that's what they'll get," was the attitude Johnson adopted.

His next big step was to establish the American League as a second major league by putting teams in several big eastern cities where they competed directly with National League teams. McGraw, who had also become dissatisfied with the National League, was given an American League franchise in Baltimore. Connie Mack—without a ball park, with few funds, but with more than enough confidence and courage—moved into Philadelphia. Hugh Duffy replaced him at Milwaukee. The American League also put teams in Boston and Washington. Before long many of the prominent National League players were jumping to the Johnson circuit.

17. A Close Call

The National League continued to be in bad shape during the first two years of the new century. The internal fighting, the battle with the American League, and a big drop in attendance all added to its troubles. The owners were in a desperate mood.

During the summer of 1901 Andrew Freedman and three others hatched an incredible plan to solve their difficulties. Freedman was a stubborn, ruthless man

with a special talent for making enemies. As owner of the controlling interest in the New York Giants, he had defied the National League, the players, the fans—anyone who opposed him.

Freedman's answer to the problems of the National League was to turn the organization into a trust. This corporation or syndicate could control every aspect of the game. There would be one owner instead of eight. Franchises and

41

players could easily be shifted wherever and whenever it would do the corporation the most good. Competition among the teams, of course, would become a farce. But Freedman and his friends didn't care about that. They were interested only in making a profit.

A sports writer somehow learned of the plot and printed the whole story. Once the news was out, the four owners who had not conspired with Freedman demanded a showdown.

It came during the League's winter meetings in New York. Barney Dreyfuss, owner of the Pirates, insisted that the League elect a new president.

"I nominate Al Spalding," he said.

This startled the Freedman group, since Spalding was in retirement.

They recovered quickly, however, and cast four votes against Spalding. The other four voted for Spalding.

Spalding's name was put to a vote again. The results were the same. Four votes for Spalding, four against.

There was a great deal of argument as the voting went on. Finally the meeting broke up, and both sides vowed to settle the matter the next day.

As the eight owners and Nick Young, the National League president, gathered together in the meeting room to resume the voting, the door opened quietly. To the amazement of the Freedman group, in walked Al Spalding.

"Good morning, gentlemen," Spalding said. "I've come to talk to you about the future of baseball." Spalding, an eloquent and forceful speaker, proceeded to appeal to the owners not to syndicate baseball.

Albert G. Spalding

"Such a move would mean the ruination of the game," he said.

When he was finished, Spalding left as quickly and quietly as he had entered. He then called a press conference. First he produced documents that confirmed the plot to turn the League into a syndicate. The syndicate, according to the plans, was to be run by a board of five managers, headed by a president.

In strong and plain language, Spalding made his views clear. There must be no syndication of baseball, he insisted, because such a system would mean that ". . . one man or half a dozen men might dominate the entire business —and with villainous brutality. . . ." Then Spalding went on to say that Freedman, if elected president, would have to quit baseball "because . . . on his baseball record, I say Freedman is more kinds of a fool than ever before existed in baseball."

It was a clever move on Spalding's part, for it brought great press and public pressure to bear on the Freedman forces. But still the matter of a new president of the National League had to be resolved.

The balloting resumed. This time Nick Young was nominated for reëlection. Time after time, however, the balloting results were the same: four votes for Spalding, four votes for Young.

Finally Freedman and his supporters became exhausted. They made a motion to adjourn the meeting. The motion went to a vote. The results? Four to four!

Completely out of patience, Freedman and his friends left the meeting room, empowering Young to vote for them. Soon, however, Young could stay awake no longer.

"The meeting is adjourned," he said. Since there was no quorum, he was sure no business could be transacted in his absence.

He was wrong.

John Rogers, owner of the Philadelphia club, was voted to the chair. Then a strange thing happened. A man named Knowles, who was Freedman's secretary, put his head in the meeting-room door. He apparently wanted to see what was going on and report back to his boss.

John Rogers quickly announced:

"With F. M. Knowles of the New York Giants present, we now have a quorum. Proceed with the voting for president."

Although Knowles quickly withdrew, Al Spalding was elected president of the National League on the twenty-sixth ballot by a vote of 4 to 0.

By that time it was after 1:00 A.M. on a Saturday morning. Rogers and his three companions awakened Spalding and told him the news.

"All right boys," Spalding said. "If that's the way you want it I'll go along. One thing, though—we must get possession of the League records. I saw them in a large trunk under a table in the meeting room."

At 4:00 A.M., Spalding roused Nick Young, told him he was the new president, and demanded the League records. Young refused. While the two men argued, two hotel porters slipped into the meeting room, picked up the trunk, and carried it to Spalding's quarters.

The next day Spalding called another press conference. He told an excited group of sports writers he was the newly elected president of the National League and outlined some broad plans for improvement of the League. In closing, Spalding commented that he assumed his election meant that Freedman was out of baseball.

Freedman, hot with anger at the turn of events, was not quite out of baseball, however. He secured a court injunction to prevent Spalding from taking office.

Spalding was too fast. He got out of the state before the papers could be served. Finally the Freedman faction knew it was licked. Freedman gave up his interest in the Giants. As soon as that happened, Spalding resigned.

Baseball had, indeed, been saved.

43

18. Peace! It's Wonderful!

Shortly after the start of the new century, baseball began to enjoy a prosperity it had never known before. There were several reasons for this. First, the leagues had finally become stable, and they were working together. At the annual meetings of 1902 and 1903, the National and American leagues buried the hatchet. A new agreement was drawn up to cover both the major and minor leagues. It also established the important player and territorial rights so essential to the orderly conduct of the game. By the end of 1902 the American League was located in Chicago, Cleveland, St. Louis, New York, Detroit, Boston, Washington, and Philadelphia. There were no more changes for half a century.

The rule makers had also finally found the proper balance between offense and defense. And, perhaps most important of all, a host of exciting new names and personalities appeared. Combined, these factors produced thrilling pennant races. They also built up intercity rivalries and won back the confidence of the public.

Among the "greats" of the era was a big, raw-boned rookie named John Peter Wagner, who came to be known as "Hans," then "Honus." Wagner broke into professional baseball in 1895 in the Michigan State League. He moved to Paterson of the Atlantic League for the next two years, then made the jump to the major leagues, signing with Louisville. In 1900, however, the Louisville Club was owned by the same man who held the Pittsburgh franchise. The Louisville team was broken up, and its best players were moved to Pittsburgh. Among them was Wagner.

Wagner looked like anything but a ball player. He was square of build and slightly bow-legged. A huge pair of hands dangled from long, powerful arms. When he moved, he looked like a big bear.

But Wagner, like King Kelly before him, could do anything on the diamond. During the early part of his career, he played every position. He pitched, caught, played the outfield and infield. In 1902, however, Pittsburgh's playing manager, Fred Clarke, stationed Wagner at shortstop. And there he stayed until 1917, playing 2,785 games, a League record.

With Wagner and Clarke starring in the field and at bat, the Pittsburgh Pirates won three straight pennants, beginning with 1901.

In 1904, Christy Mathewson, another all-time great, burst upon the baseball world. In the course of his 16-year period in the majors, Mathewson won 373 games. Many say he was the game's best pitcher.

Mathewson started in professional ball in 1899, with a salary of $90 a month. After a year in the New England League, he moved to Norfolk. He had a trial with the Giants, but lost his first three games and was sent back to Norfolk by Andrew Freedman. Mathewson was not disturbed by his showing with

Honus Wagner (below), the raw-boned Pittsburgh shortstop who could do almost anything on the diamond.

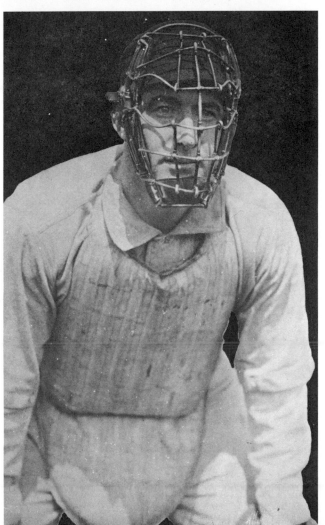

Both pitcher Christy Mathewson (upper right) and catcher Roger Bresnahan (left) won fame as Giant stars.

45

the Giants. He went on to win 21 games at Norfolk, while losing but two. He was drafted by Cincinnati, then traded back to the Giants.

Mathewson started off with a bang. The second time he put on his Giant uniform, he won eight in a row, four by shut-outs. In his ninth appearance, he lost 1-0. By the end of the season, he had appeared in 40 games, pitching more than 300 innings. He had 20 victories to his credit, including one no-hit game.

In 1902 Mathewson became one of the first pitchers of the new era to win 30 games. In each of the following two years he won the same number.

Another Giant pitcher who made history in the early 1900s was Joe McGinnity. In 1903 he pitched in 55 games, winning 31 and losing 19. Three times during August, McGinnity pitched both games in double-headers. And he won them all!

The Giant's catcher, Roger Bresnahan, was another remarkable performer of the period. Few catchers in all the history of the game can compare with Bresnahan. He was a tough fighter, exceptionally fast on the base paths, and a powerful hitter. He also satisfied Giant manager John McGraw, the old Oriole star, with the way he ran the defense—something few players could do. (Bresnahan is credited with being the first catcher to wear shin guards.)

One of the most remarkable pitchers of that day was George Edward Waddell, a six-foot, three-inch giant. Waddell, called "Rube" by everyone, was an utter child. At the slightest provocation

"Rube" Waddell, Connie Mack's remarkable but unreliable pitcher.

he would wander off the field. Once, just as he was to take the mound, a fire engine went clanging by the ball park. Waddell immediately took off after it.

Waddell was eccentric and unreliable, for sure. But, oh, how he could pitch! He had to wander about the minor leagues for a long time, however, before a major-league manager would take a chance on him. The first and only manager who could handle the childish pitcher was Connie Mack. And even Mack didn't have an easy time of it.

Mack first heard of Waddell while managing the Milwaukee team. Needing another strong pitcher, he sent for the big-shouldered Rube, who was playing semi-professional ball in Pennsylvania. For almost two weeks Mack sent a daily telegram to Rube, offering him a job with Milwaukee. Finally the pitcher responded by a telegram.

"Come and get me," it said.

Mack did just that. To get Waddell out of town, however, he had to pay some of the pitcher's debts and rescue his belongings from a hock shop.

Some of Waddell's most memorable games were against the redoubtable Cy Young. On May 5, 1904, Young beat Waddell by hurling a perfect game. The next year Waddell beat Young in a 3–2 thriller that went to 20 innings.

Mack often said that Waddell—with a burning fast ball and a big curve that traveled at about the same speed—had more natural throwing ability than any pitcher he had ever seen. He was probably right.

Mack was blessed with other fine pitchers in the 1900s. One of them was Edward Stewart Plank, a left-hander. Mack found Plank on the campus of Gettysburg College. Plank was one of the few lefties to win 300 or more games.

Mordecai Peter Centennial Brown of the Chicago Cubs was still another pitcher who drew nation-wide attention. While working on a farm during his youth, Brown had lost the index finger of his throwing hand. The finger next to it was also badly maimed. As a result, he was known as "Three Finger" Brown.

In the midst of one of baseball's bitterest rivalries, Brown and the great Christy Mathewson had a remarkable series of pitching duels. In June of 1905, for instance, Brown and Mathewson matched each other pitch for pitch throughout nine innings. Neither side got a hit or a run. Finally Brown weakened and surrendered two hits. The Giants won 1-0.

Following that defeat, however, the Chicago Cubs, with Brown on the mound, beat Mathewson nine straight. Brown and Mathewson pitched against each other 24 times over a 13-year period with Brown winning 13 of the games.

19. The One-Run Days

The baseball used in the first decade of this century had less bounce per foot than any employed before or since. Hitters couldn't drive the ball very far, and one run was often the difference between victory and defeat.

The old-timers say the dead-ball days were the best because the team at bat had to vary its attack in order to get a run. The players had to steal, bunt, and use the hit-and-run and squeeze plays much more often than today. The oldsters also point out that, in today's game, one blow by the weakest hitter on the team can bring a pitcher's battle to a quick end.

Other fans are opposed to the one-run game because it gives the pitcher too powerful a role in the contest.

Whatever the answer may be, baseball was obviously a mighty thrilling spectacle between 1900 and 1910. And that is just about how long the dead ball lasted.

In 1904, for example, the New York Highlanders were in a neck-and-neck battle with the Boston Red Sox. On the last day of the season, the teams met in a double-header at the Polo Grounds. A split of the games would mean a tie. To win the pennant, the Highlanders needed to take both.

With Jack Chesbro on the mound for the first game, the Highlanders' chances looked promising.

But Chesbro had his hands full. When he strode from the dugout to start the ninth inning, the score was tied at 2–2. Red Sox catcher Lou Criger opened with a single. A sacrifice bunt put him on second base. An infield out moved him to third.

Chesbro needed only one out to get out of the inning. His next pitch, however, bounded past the catcher and Criger scored what proved to be the winning run. For years fans said it was the costliest wild pitch ever unfurled by a moundsman.

The Red Sox fans, still tingling over their victory against the Highlanders, looked forward to a championship series with the New York Giants, managed by John McGraw. The Giants were the winners of the National League pennant. But Giant owner John Brush still carried a grudge against Ban Johnson and would have no part of such a championship game.

"The American League is still bush," was the attitude of Brush and his manager, John McGraw. "They're not in a class with the Giants."

Such disdainful treatment of the Red Sox and the American League in general aroused a storm of protest. All was smoothed over at the winter meetings, however. Both leagues decided it would be profitable and wise to arrange an annual series between the winners of each league. And that's how the World Series—inaugurated in 1905—was officially established.

A fiction writer couldn't have made the first modern World Series more dramatic. McGraw's Giants, with Mathew-

The New York Highlanders—later to become the Yankees—play the Philadelphia Athletics at the Polo Grounds in 1907.

Frank Chance, first baseman and manager of the Chicago Cubs.

hanging out the train window on the return trip to Philadelphia. With Waddell on the sidelines, Mathewson dominated the series. Over a period of six days, Matty pitched three games against the Athletics. He won them all by shut-outs. During the 27 scoreless innings, Matty gave up 14 hits and struck out 18 Athletics, one of them five times. He walked but one man.

The Giants made McGraw look good by taking the Series four games to one.

The Giants didn't win the next year, though. Starting in 1906, the remarkable Chicago Cubs won the flag in four out of five campaigns.

The Cubs, along with Three Finger Brown, had a fine infield. Their double-play combination included shortstop

One of the all-time greats, Ty Cobb, demonstrates his famous batting grip.

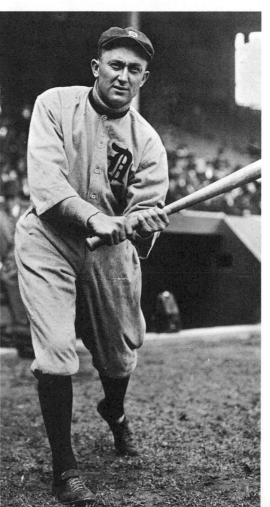

son, McGinnity, and Bresnahan turning in one glittering performance after another, won the National pennant again.

In the American League, Connie Mack's strong mound corps of Waddell, Plank, and Bender gave the Athletics the flag. Although the fans looked forward to watching gentle Connie Mack match wits with the fiery McGraw, they wanted most of all to see what would happen when Waddell and Mathewson met.

Waddell never made the World Series that year. The Rube injured his shoulder—not on the ball diamond, but in a wrestling match at the Boston railroad station. Rube fell heavily on his pitching shoulder, then slept with his arm

Joe Tinker, second baseman John Evers and first baseman and manager Frank Chance. So many times did this trio thwart Giant rallies that the witty Franklin P. Adams wrote that the saddest possible words on the diamond were—

"Tinker to Evers to Chance."

While the Cubs roared through the National League to set a 1906 record of 116 victories, the Chicago White Sox won in the American League. Although dubbed the "hitless wonders" because they batted an anemic .228, the White Sox defeated the Cubs in World Series play by a score of 4 games to 2.

In moving toward the pennant, the White Sox had to squeeze past the Athletics and a new powerhouse—the Detroit Tigers. The Tiger lineup included an outfielder baseball fans would be hearing more about—Tyrus Raymond Cobb.

During his 24 years in the Big Leagues, the Tiger outfielder collected 4,191 base hits for a lifetime batting average of .367. No player who has been in major-league baseball for 10 years or more can come close to that record.

Cobb first won the American League batting title in 1907. He won it 11 more times, 9 in succession. On three occasions his average was over .400. Only one other modern player—Rogers Hornsby—equaled that record.

Cobb was the first player elected to baseball's Hall of Fame. Many consider him the greatest player of all time. It's hard to believe, but 16 of the many records set by Cobb still stand. Some of them, like his record of 829 stolen bases, may never be broken. Of course, records alone never give a full picture of a player or a team. This was particularly true in the case of Ty Cobb, one of baseball's most daring and fearless ball players.

20. The Merkle Incident

In their wildest dreams, ball fans could not have imagined what was in store for them during the 1908 season. In the American League three teams— the Cleveland Naps, the Detroit Tigers, and the Chicago White Sox—fought it out right down to the *last day* of the season. Then, by beating Chicago, Detroit nosed out Cleveland by a half a game.

Before that spectacular finish, however, White Sox pitcher Edward A. Walsh had put on an astounding show.

He appeared in 66 games, started 55, and finished all but six. At the close of the season, he had 40 victories to his credit, as against 15 losses.

That same season Ed Reulbach of the Chicago Cubs drew almost as much comment as Walsh. In the National League the Cubs were fighting a fierce three-cornered battle with the New York Giants and Pittsburgh Pirates. At one point in the contest, Reulbach hurled 44 scoreless innings, a feat that went un-

matched until 1933. In the midst of that string, he shut out Brooklyn in a double-header by scores of 5–0 and 3–0.

Reulbach's toil might have gone for naught, however, had it not been for the heads-up play of teammate Johnny Evers. The Chicago second baseman, alert and persistent, touched off an incident that will live in baseball history books forever.

To appreciate what happened, one must go back to September 4 of that memorable season and review one play that took place in a game between the Cubs and Pirates at Pittsburgh.

It was the bottom of the tenth inning. Neither the Pirates nor the Cubs had scored. But Pirate manager Fred Clarke was on third base, with Warren Gill on first. At bat stood the Flying Dutchman, Honus Wagner.

Wagner, always tough when runners were on base, slammed a drive to center field. Clarke easily made it home. Warren Gill, noting that Clarke had crossed the plate, didn't bother to touch second. He thought the game was over, so he ran to the clubhouse.

But Johnny Evers called to center fielder Art Hofman:

"Throw me the ball, Art!"

Hofman made the toss to Evers. Evers stepped on second.

"That run doesn't count," Evers complained to umpire Hank O'Day. "Gill is out."

Evers was perfectly right. The rule covering the play says:

"A run is not scored if the runner advances to home base during a play in which the third out is made (1) by the batter-runner before he touches first base; (2) by a runner being forced out . . ."

To the dismay of Evers and his Cub mates, however, umpire O'Day said brusquely:

"I didn't see it, so I can't call it."

Cub owner Charles Webb Murphy promptly filed a protest with the League, but it was disallowed. The Cubs, bitterly disappointed, not only lost the ball game, but dropped to third place in the standings.

Just 19 days later, on September 23, the identical situation arose in a game with the Giants at the Polo Grounds. It was the third game of a four-game series. The Cubs had won the first two and the Giants were trying desperately to even things. The score was tied at 1-1 as the Giants came to bat in the last half of the ninth inning. There are different versions of what actually happened next, but the following is believed to be fairly accurate.

A Giant player named Devlin got the first hit of the inning, a single to left field. Then Moose McCormick grounded to the infield, forcing Devlin to second. Devlin went into the bag so hard he upset second baseman Evers, preventing the possibility of a double play.

A fight started at second base, but was quickly broken up by the umpires. Devlin was out.

The next Giant hitter was Fred Merkle, a quiet, modest player who showed great promise. It was his second year in the majors.

Merkle powdered the ball to deep center, and the crowd roared as Mc-

Joe Tinker (upper left) and Johnny Evers (lower left) were an important two-thirds of the famous Chicago Cub trio — Tinker-Evers-Chance.

53

Cormick streaked around the bases. He had a chance to score and end the game —or so it seemed. Cub outfielder Jack Hayden cut the ball off on a fine play and made a good throw to the infield. McCormick had to hold at third, leaving Merkle at first.

With Giant fans hooting and yelling encouragement, Al Birdwell singled sharply to center field when he came up to bat. Umpire Emslie, standing in back of second base, dropped to the ground to avoid being hit by the ball.

McCormick, of course, crossed home plate. As he did so, the gleeful Giant fans, sure their favorites had won the game, poured from their seats.

But like Pittsburgh's Warren Gill, Merkle failed to touch second. Instead he raced for the clubhouse.

Heady Johnny Evers again stepped on second and yelled to Hofman in center field.

"Throw it here! Throw it here!"

Hofman threw, but the ball got away from Evers. It rolled into the crowd surging onto the field, unaware of what was going on. Two Giants, however, must have known exactly what Evers was up to. Pitcher Floyd Kroh raced from the Giant dugout and picked up the ball. Joe McGinnity was right behind him. Before Kroh could move, McGinnity snatched the ball from Kroh's hands and heaved it into the stands.

Evers still didn't give up. He dashed to the plate and took another ball from umpire O'Day. Then he ran back to second, stepped on the bag, and insisted that Merkle was out. Umpire Emslie couldn't rule on Evers' appeal. In duck-

ing away from Birdwell's hit, he had been unable to watch Merkle. This left it up to Hank O'Day.

"What do ya say, Hank?" Merkle shouted above the noise of the screaming crowd.

"Merkle is out!" was O'Day's prompt reply. He then declared the game a tie and suspended play.

The few Giant fans who realized what had happened threatened O'Day. He had to have police protection to get to his dressing room.

The next day the president of the League upheld O'Day's ruling. The Giants quickly lodged a protest and asked for a hearing. The Cubs, to add a little more fuel to the fire, arrived at the Polo Grounds two hours earlier than the time scheduled for the fourth game of the series.

Their purpose?

"Under the rules we should play off yesterday's tie game today," Manager Chance explained to the sports writers. "And since the Giants aren't here, we claim we win by forfeiture."

The League now had *two* thorny problems to handle!

The crowd arriving with the Giants that day was in such a belligerent mood the police wouldn't permit anyone to sit close to the outfield. When the game was over, however, the Giant fans were happier. Their beloved Christy Mathewson had whipped the hateful Cubs 5 to 4.

A New York *Times* reporter gave the stay-at-homes a glimpse of the way things were at the ball park when he wrote:

In the early 1900s a Giant fan could see the games free if he was good at tree-climbing.

"Everybody slaps everybody else and nobody minds. Perfect ladies are screaming like a batch of Coney barkers on the Mardi Gras occasion and the elderly banker behind us is beating our hat to a pulp with a gold-headed cane, but nobody minds. The merry villagers flock on the field to worship the hollow where the Mathewson feet have pressed . . ."

The National League officials apparently felt that there was little chance of a tie finish in the 1908 pennant race. At least they made no move to rule on the winner of the September 23 game between the Giants and Cubs.

Later on, to everyone's astonishment, the Giants, Cubs and Pirates appeared to be heading for a triple tie! Thus, just before the season ended, the League faced up to the fact that it had to make a decision about the Merkle affair.

21. Climax!

For two days and the greater part of one night, three National League directors listened to arguments and evidence presented by the Giants and Cubs concerning the September 23 game. Finally the weary League officials ruled that Merkle was out when he failed to touch second base in the ninth inning of the game in dispute. Thus the score was 1–1. The Cubs' claim of a forfeiture was disallowed. If the tie had a bearing on the final standings, it would have to be replayed at the end of the season.

The day before the last day of the season, it became obvious that the September 23 game would have to be replayed. For on the last day the Giants were scheduled to play Boston at Boston. A victory for New York would mean a tie between the Giants and Cubs. A victory for Boston would mean a tie among the Giants, Cubs, and Pirates.

So regardless of how the Boston-Giant game ended, the replay of the 1–1 September game would have to take place.

On October 7 hundreds of Chicago fans saw the Cubs off as they boarded a special car attached to the Twentieth Century Limited. At Elkhart, Indiana— the first stop—hundreds more swarmed about the train, cheering the Cubs wildly. At departure time they refused to let the train go until Three Finger Brown, the Cubs' star hurler, went to the platform to say a few words.

As Brown finished speaking, the Elkhart station master rushed out of the station waving a piece of telegraph ticker tape.

"The Giants beat Boston! The Giants beat Boston!" he yelled.

The crowd whooped. The Twentieth Century tooted. The Cubs were off to New York for one of the most fateful games in the history of baseball.

The excitement that gripped New York as game time drew nearer and nearer was unprecedented. In the darkness of the preceding night, a dozen fans slipped into the Polo Grounds, hid among the seats, and awaited the call of "Play Ball!"

Shortly after daylight, thousands of fans from the city proper, as well as from surrounding areas, began the long trek to the Polo Grounds. A great mass of humanity—at least 80,000 and probably 100,000—tried to jam its way through the streets and into the grounds. At that time the stands seated no more than about 35,000.

Police were rushed to the area from every section of the city, but they could not control the hordes of people.

As one reporter described it:

"Thousands piled upon thousands in a fearful tangle . . . the police were swept aside like corks before a torrent. And the horses of the mounted men were pushed and jammed against the walls surrounding the grounds. . . ."

Scores of men and boys clambered over the 15-foot outfield fences, undaunted by the three strands of barbed wire that topped them. Hundreds climbed to the roof of the stands. (Two fell to the ground and were seriously injured.) Additional hundreds lined the tracks of the elevated electric trains that ran near the park.

Some spectators even scrambled up the sides of the elevated trains and sat atop them. When they wouldn't get off, the trainmen slowly moved the trains to the next station.

Excitement ran so high during the 1908 Series that the crowds broke through the fences at the Polo Grounds.

Mordecai "Three Finger" Brown, star hurler for the Cubs.

Fred Merkle, the Giant rookie who touched off the famous 1908 "incident."

According to newspaper reports of the day, several men sat along the thin, upper edge of a huge billboard that loomed above the elevated tracks. And there was a man atop each of the several thin, steel signal towers near the field. The towers were 100 feet tall.

Excitement was running high on the diamond, too. As the bell rang, ending batting practice for the Cubs, Joe McGinnity and Frank Chance became em-

broiled in a hot argument. McGinnity rapped Chance on the chin. Chance retaliated, but others stepped in and separated the two.

Christy Mathewson, pitching for the Giants against Three Finger Brown, seemed in superb form as the game started.

As the fans screamed, "The fadeaway, Matty! The fadeaway!" he whiffed the first six batters he faced. But the determined Cubs rocked him in the third inning with a four-run outburst. The Giants could get only two runs from Brown.

As a result of the play-off the Cubs became the 1908 National League champions. They left the field amid a shower of pop bottles, thrown by the disappointed New York Giant fans.

In the clubhouse Merkle wept with shame. Over and over again he said to Giant manager McGraw:

"Get rid of me, Mac! Get rid of me! I don't deserve to play with the Giants!"

But McGraw, toughest of the tough, a manager who was supposed to be heartless, patted Merkle on the shoulder and said gruffly:

"Forget it, Fred. As of right now you've got a $500 raise."

For years afterward, however, the fans hooted at Merkle when he appeared on the field. And whenever anyone made a foolish mistake, it was often referred to as "a Merkle."

22. The Big Train

The pennant races of 1908, torrid as they were, didn't capture all the headlines that memorable year. As always, there were a number of remarkable individual performances.

The most amazing of these was turned in by a pitcher for the seventh-place Washington Senators, Walter Perry Johnson.

Johnson, rounding out his first full year in the majors, shut out the Highlanders 3–0 on September 4, a Friday. He also shut them out on Saturday, 6–0. Since the law didn't permit the playing of professional ball on Sunday, the teams were idle. On Monday Johnson was back on the mound for the final game of the series. This time he whipped New York 4–0. In all, Johnson had given up but 12 hits. On September 11 he pitched

"No mere mortal" could throw a baseball as hard as the newcomer from Idaho—Walter P. Johnson.

59

the Senators to a 2–1 victory over the Athletics. The next day, he beat them again by a 5–4 score.

When Johnson had arrived in Washington during August of 1907, he was not unknown. No one can strike out an average of 20 batters a game, as Johnson did in the Idaho State League, without attracting attention. The stories circulated about Johnson, however, were so extravagant with praise that few believed them.

Even those who saw him make his debut with the Senators scarcely trusted their senses. As one awed sports reporter wrote:

"No mere mortal can throw a baseball as hard as the newcomer from Idaho. I have seen him pitch, but I do not believe what I have seen. My eyes speak falsehoods."

In a way, Johnson's great speed caused him to lose his first game for the Senators. The opposing Detroit Tigers, unable to hit his lightning-like deliveries, cleverly resorted to bunting and were able to eke out a 3–2 victory.

Ty Cobb, who led the attack against Johnson that day, said later:

"The most terrible experience in baseball is to visit Washington on a cloudy day when Johnson is pitching."

On another occasion, after striking out against Johnson, Cobb muttered:

"You can't hit what you can't see."

In 21 seasons, Walter Johnson established 15 American League records—more than any other pitcher. These included the most games won (413), the most shutouts (113), the most innings pitched (5,925) and the most consecutive scoreless innings (56).

Johnson, a powerful square-shouldered man with strong features, was likened to the giant steam locomotives of his day.

"The Big Train is coming to town," wrote a sports writer when Johnson and the Senators traveled to New York. And "The Big Train" he remained to all as he rolled on, year after glorious year.

23. Color and Competition

One might think that interest in baseball would have faded after a year like 1908. Actually the turnstiles spun at a merrier rate than ever for the next several seasons.

There were many reasons for this. First of all, the American and National League franchises were left undisturbed. This gave the teams a chance to build a loyal home following which, in turn, led to intense rivalries between cities.

As fan interest grew, so did the prestige of baseball. In 1910 William Howard Taft became the first President of the United States to toss out the ball that opened the season. The President and all the other Washington rooters were thrilled by Walter Johnson's per-

William Howard Taft, the first President of the United States to toss out the season's opening ball.

formance that day. He just missed pitching a no-hit game. Taft became an outspoken admirer of Johnson, as did Presidents Harding and Wilson in later years.

Although still poorly paid, the players responded to the rooting of their loyal followers by putting on a spectacular show. The Cincinnati Reds, for example, stole 310 bases in 1910 even though the manufacturers had added cork to the center of the baseball to make it more lively. The Reds' leading base stealer was Bob Bescher with a record of 80. The National League, as a whole, recorded 1,691 stolen bases!

Ty Cobb led the American League with 76 stolen bases. But despite the efforts of Cobb and Bescher, neither the Tigers nor the Reds won pennants that year.

Instead, the American League championship was taken by the Athletics, who won 102 games. The Athletics were the first American League team to go over the 100-win mark. In fact in 1910 they were one of the finest teams in baseball. Brilliant Eddie Collins led the A's attack with a .322 batting average and 67 stolen bases (second to Cobb).

Collins was also the middle man in baseball's best infield. Referred to as the "$100,000 infield," it included Frank Baker, Stuffy McInnis, Jack Barry, and Harry Davis.

The pitching, too, was very strong. Together, Jack Coombs and Charles "Chief" Bender won 54 games. Coombs had 13 shutouts among his 31 victories. Eddie Plank, although getting along in years, won 16 games.

The Cubs won the National League pennant, but they were no match for the Athletics in the 1910 World Series play. They lost by a score of 4–1.

The following year the Giants virtually "stole" the pennant by stealing a record total of 347 bases. Such a display of footwork is not without hazard, however. As the season progressed, the Giants' uniforms became more and more tattered and worn. Finally, during a game in Chicago, it happened. A Giant slid into second and couldn't get up. His pants were no longer on his body. A cordon of teammates led him from the field to the whooping delight of the fans.

That same year, 1911, Ty Cobb led the American League again with 83 stolen bases. He also batted a phenomenal .420 and scored 147 runs. Still his team couldn't match the Athletics. The Tigers trailed by 13½ games. The Athletics had a .400 hitter of their own that year—Shoeless Joe Jackson. Jackson, one of the best hitters ever to grace the diamond, batted .411.

When the Giants and Athletics met in the World Series, the fans became conscious of a new weapon of attack—the home run.

It didn't show itself in the first game when the Giants bested the Athletics 2–1 in a bitterly fought contest. But in the second game it exploded against Rube Marquard. Marquard, who had won 24 games for the Giants, gave up but four hits during the game. But unfortunately one of them was the homer which rang off the bat of Frank Baker, giving the ball game to the Athletics.

The Giants' Christy Mathewson and

In 1910-11 nobody in the American League managed to steal more bases than Ty Cobb.

the Athletics' Jack Coombs dueled away in the third game. In the ninth inning, with the score tied at 1–1, Baker came to bat. Matty, working carefully, slipped two strikes past the third baseman. He wound up and fired again.

Baker swung and seemed to miss the ball. But the umpire ruled that Baker's bat had touched it. This gave Baker another chance. He promptly belted Matty's next pitch into the stands. Although the Giants evened matters in the bottom of the ninth, they lost in the eleventh

when the A's scored another run.

The Athletics went on to win the Series. Baker's unheard-of feat—hitting two round-trippers in the Series—earned for him the nickname "Home Run Baker."

In 1912 the pennant races continued to whet the fans' appetite for baseball, especially in the American League. Ty Cobb, hated as much as admired, drew cheers and jeers in an ever rising crescendo. The jeers finally got out of hand. In a hotly fought series in New York on May 15, Cobb astounded everyone by

63

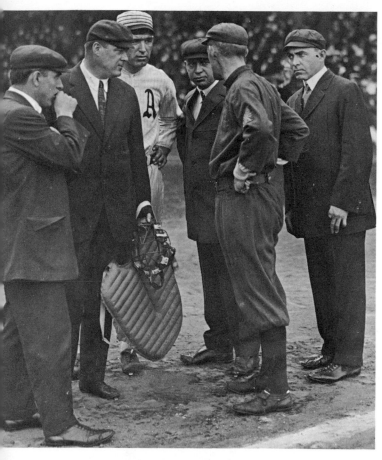

The captains of the Braves and Athletics have a conference with the umpires at the start of the 1914 World Series.

leaping into the stands to grab a fan by the throat and pummel him.

"He insulted me," Cobb explained later.

This didn't satisfy Ban Johnson, who sent a wire to the Detroit management: "Cobb suspended indefinitely."

Cobb's teammates, knowing what he meant to the club, sent a telegram back to Johnson. They said they would strike if Cobb's suspension wasn't lifted.

Johnson, never one to be bluffed, had a ready reply. If the players struck, Detroit would be fined $5,000 for each game not played.

The players struck anyway when the team was scheduled to play in Philadelphia. Hughie Jennings, the manager, to keep the schedule, put himself into the lineup along with his coaches and a group of college players. The game was a farce, of course. The Athletics won 24–2.

The next day's game was canceled, but Cobb begged his mates to resume playing, which they did. Each man who signed the telegram was fined $100, while Cobb's suspension lasted 10 days and was capped by a $50 fine.

Meanwhile, the Boston Red Sox and Washington Senators were stirring up even more excitement in the American League.

Walter Johnson, pitching for a relatively weak team, won 32 games while losing 16. During one stretch he won 16 in a row as the Senators moved from sixth place to second.

The Boston club, a real powerhouse, rolled up 104 wins to take the flag. Boston pitcher Smoky Joe Wood also won 16 in a row that year and wound up with a total of 34 wins and 5 losses. Unlike Johnson, Wood had the backing of a remarkable outfield in Tris Speaker, Duffy Lewis, and Harry Hooper. This trio could field and hit with the best that baseball has ever seen.

In the National League, meanwhile, John McGraw's Giants won still another pennant. The World Series was a great climax to the season, with the Red Sox winning 4–3.

The following year Connie Mack added two remarkable rookies to his pitching staff—Bullet Joe Bush and Herb Pennock. The additions meant another Athletic pennant.

The still superb Christy Mathewson and Rube Marquard (who won 19 in a row) led the Giants to the flag in the National League. But in the World Series play the A's again downed the Giants, this time 4–1. The lone Giant victory went to Mathewson.

The Athletics repeated their pennant victory in 1914, but they didn't have such an easy time in the World Series. Instead of the Giants, they encountered a "miracle team," the Boston Braves.

Managed by George Stallings, the Braves astounded everyone by moving from last place in mid-July to a pennant victory in September.

The Braves, a "hot" ball club, rolled over the A's in four straight games, the first time this had ever been accomplished in World Series play.

The star of the Series was the Braves' Hank Gowdy, who batted .545 with a homer, triple, and three doubles. He also collected six walks from the jittery Athletic pitchers.

The close of the 1914 season marked the climax of a prosperous era. Intercity rivalries and color and competition had made it so.

24. The "Feds"

In 1913 baseball's comfortable financial position suddenly began to be threatened from several directions at once. Some two million Americans were spending their free time with a noisy, unreliable contraption called a motor car, or "horseless buggy." Thousands of others were drawn to the "electric theater," where they could watch moving pictures tell fascinating stories.

Still more serious was the formation of the Federal League by a group of wealthy businessmen. Within three months, the Feds built eight new ball parks. Many were in cities where the National and American League teams had franchises.

To get players, the Federal League owners followed the patterns of the past. They offered the established stars more money than they were receiving. Three Finger Brown, Joe Tinker, Ed Reulbach and Hal Chase were among many who jumped to the Federal League.

Surprisingly enough, the Feds put on a fine show in 1914, their first season. Indianapolis nosed out Chicago for the pennant, but every team was in contention at one time or another. The closeness of the race drew big crowds.

Encouraged by such a fine start, the Federals got bolder in 1915 and moved the Indianapolis franchise to Newark. They also continued to lure players from

*Charles "Chief" Bender, one of the Athletics'
star pitchers, transferred to the new Federal
League in 1915.*

By the time the Boston Red Sox met Philadelphia of the National League in the World Series, there were reports that the Federals were going to move into New York for 1916. Because of all the competition from automobiles, movies, and the Federal League, attendance had fallen off for the first time in years.

Just when things were blackest, the Federal League owners—men used to getting their own way—had a quarrel. Then their richest and most powerful member, Robert Ward, died unexpectedly.

The American and National Leagues quickly bid for peace. After a number of conferences, they bought out the Federal League franchises, throwing the players on the open market.

Two important ownership changes followed the breakup of the Federal League. One of the Federal owners—Charles Weeghman—bought the Chicago Cubs, then built Wrigley Field for them.

In New York two colonels—Jacob Ruppert and Tillinghast L'Hommedieu Huston—purchased the American League team known as the Highlanders. The Highlanders, however, were soon to become much better known under a new name, The Yankees.

the National and American loops, including Chief Bender and Eddie Plank.

The flag chase that year was even more exciting than the year before. Chicago, St. Louis, and Pittsburgh fought it out right down to the wire with the rest of the League close behind. Chicago won by one percentage point.

25. From White to Black

World War I had an inevitable effect on baseball. Many of the leading ball players joined the ranks of the doughboys sailing for the battlefront in France. Even so, baseball was able to continue. And in 1918, during the closing months of the war, the Boston Red Sox whipped the Chicago Cubs 4–2 in World Series play.

By the spring of 1919, baseball, like the rest of the world, began to get back to normal. The Chicago White Sox, boasting the most powerful lineup in the major leagues, rolled easily to a pennant in the American League, while a less imposing club, the Cincinnati Reds, took the National League flag.

Ed Cicotte was the leading pitcher of the White Sox with 29 victories and 7 losses. Others who contributed heavily to the championship drive of the Chicago team were Ray Schalk, catcher, outfielders Shoeless Joe Jackson and Oscar "Happy" Felsch, and pitchers Claude "Lefty" Williams and Dickie Kerr. Then there was Charles "Swede" Risberg at shortstop, Chick Gandil, first baseman, and George "Buck" Weaver, third baseman. Pilot of the Sox was William "Kid" Gleason, a member of the original Baltimore Orioles.

As Cincinnati and Chicago squared off for the best-of-nine series in Cincinnati, baseball fans were startled to learn that the Reds were favored to win the opening game and the Series. Many of the reporters who were in Cincinnati to begin coverage of the Series immediately became suspicious, not only because the Reds were favored, but also because known gamblers were circulating through the lobby of the White Sox' hotel, trying to find anyone willing to bet on Chicago.

Long before game time, there were ominous whispers.

"The Series is fixed," was the word among those who knew.

In the first game, the talented Cicotte was matched against the Reds' ace hurler, Dutch Ruether. Ruether got the Sox out without a score as the game opened. In the bottom of the first inning, however, Cicotte hit the first batter. Before the inning was over, the Reds had scored.

"What's the matter with Cicotte?" the Chicago fans wondered. "He's just lobbing the ball up there."

"He's nervous," some said aloud.

Cicotte, however, couldn't seem to settle down. In the fourth inning, the first batter flied out, the second singled, and the third was thrown out on a fielder's choice. With two outs, two singles followed, putting men on second and third. This brought to the plate the Reds' weakest hitter, pitcher Dutch Ruether.

Ruether whacked out a triple. A double and single followed, running the score to 6–1 and sending Cicotte to the showers. Before the game was over, the Reds scored three more runs and won the first game 9–1.

Kid Gleason of the White Sox had heard the whispers about a "fix" before

Record-breaking crowds thronged to watch the 1919 World Series games between the Chicago White Sox and Cincinnati Reds.

game time, but he couldn't believe them. By the end of the game he was convinced they were true. He called the players together and gave them a tongue-lashing. Later he went to owner Charles Comiskey and told him of his suspicions.

Comiskey and Gleason talked far into the night. They decided there was nothing to be done about the first game. After all, whom could they accuse? What evidence did they have?

The second game gave them little comfort, for Chicago lost again, 4–2. As the teams moved to Chicago for the third game, the "fix" rumors increased. Still Comiskey and Gleason were helpless.

Little Dickie Kerr almost made Gleason and Comiskey forget their dark suspicions. Hurling a masterful game, he whipped the Reds 3–0. The next day Cicotte begged Gleason for another chance to pitch against Cincinnati. Gleason hesitated, but finally decided to give Cicotte the assignment.

He was disappointed. Cicotte made two bad errors in the fifth inning, paving the way for a 2–0 Cincinnati victory.

Were the errors intentional, or natural?

Gleason couldn't be sure.

The fifth game was delayed a day because of rain. It was a long day for Gleason and Comiskey, tortured by the thought that their wonderful White Sox were crooked.

With Lefty Williams on the mound the next day, the White Sox lost the fifth game. Errors and all-around poor play by Felsch and Risberg gave Cincinnati the win.

The teams moved back to Cincinnati and Dick Kerr again was called on to face the Reds. He won a close one in 10 innings. Though still worried about Cicotte, Gleason asked him to pitch a third time. Cicotte was at his best. Timely hits by Jackson and Felsch gave the Sox a 4–1 victory and kept their Series hopes alive, although they trailed 4 games to 3.

The Reds crushed Chicago the next day, however, pounding Lefty Williams for four runs in the first inning. The final score was 10–5.

At the end of the Series, Charles Comiskey said he thought his players were honest. Nevertheless, he offered a $20,-000 reward for any information that could prove the Series was fixed. He also held up the Sox share of the World Series money temporarily.

No one made any attempt to claim Comiskey's reward during the winter months. By the following season the incident seemed to be forgotten.

In September, however, Chicago's Cook County Grand Jury was instructed to look into rumors that a game between the Chicago Cubs and the Philadelphia Phillies was fixed. Some of the developments touched on the Cincinnati-Chicago World Series of the year before.

Suddenly an ex-prize fighter and small-time gambler named Billy Maharg blurted out a fantastic story to a newspaperman. He said the World Series of 1919 had definitely been rigged. He named the players involved and gave facts and figures.

The Grand Jury, acting swiftly, called a number of people to testify. Unex-

White Sox player Buck Weaver out at home plate during a play of the 1919 Series.

pectedly Ed Cicotte came forward as a voluntary witness. Here, in substance, is apparently what happened:

Maharg and another man, acting upon the instructions of certain gamblers, contacted the players through first baseman Chick Gandil. They offered eight of the Sox $100,000 to lose the Series. The eight included Cicotte, Gandil, Joe Jackson, Lefty Williams, Swede Risberg, Happy Felsch, Buck Weaver and Fred McMullin.

Cicotte, who later said he needed money to pay off a mortgage on his farm, found $10,000 under his pillow after the first game. Williams, Jackson, and Felsch had been promised $20,000 each, but they received only $5,000 apiece. The others received nothing.

Shortly after Cicotte gave his story to the Grand Jury, Williams, Felsch, and Jackson told of their part in the plot. As the famous Jackson left the courthouse, a group of boys clustered about him. One, with tears streaming down his face, said:

"Say it ain't so, Joe! Say it ain't so!"

The slugging outfielder, idol of a million youngsters, flushed and hung his head. "I'm afraid it is, boys," he murmured, then hurried away.

When the ugly story broke, the Cleveland Indians were leading the Sox by one game, with three left to be played. Nonetheless, the eight implicated White Sox players were suspended. Cleveland won the pennant and the World Series, beating Brooklyn 5–2.

The Grand Jury also indicted nine players implicated in the Cubs-Phillies case. Four gamblers were indicted, too. The case didn't go to trial until the following year. At that time, it was discovered that the Grand Jury minutes, including the testimony of all the witnesses, had been stolen from the prosecutor's office.

As a result, the Grand Jury had no choice but to return a verdict of Not Guilty against all involved. Although exonerated by the court, the White Sox players were barred from baseball for life.

For years writers have been trying to unravel all that went on during the 1919 Series. Long after the incident, Ban Johnson said two groups of gamblers were involved, each trying to double-cross the other. The players were caught in between. No scandal in sports history shocked the public so much as the White Sox affair of 1919. The club owners were aware of this and decided they had better do something about it.

By coincidence August Herrmann had resigned as chairman of the National Commission, and baseball was without a supreme leader in 1920. The owners, over Ban Johnson's protests, picked Judge Kenesaw Mountain Landis as his successor. Landis was well known as a stern, courageous, and fair judge. During the war between the Federal League and the National and American Leagues, he had said:

Judge Kenesaw Mountain Landis was appointed commissioner of baseball shortly after the White Sox scandal of 1919.

"Both sides may understand that any blow at the thing called baseball would be regarded by this court as a blow to a national institution."

Landis was given the title of commissioner of baseball with a salary of $50,-000 a year. More power was put into his hands than any other baseball man had ever had.

The team owners were determined that the crookedness that changed the White Sox to the Black Sox would never happen again.

26. Rejuvenation

The severe blow dealt baseball by the Black Sox scandal was softened somewhat by the appointment of Kenesaw Mountain Landis as czar of the game. But Judge Landis wasn't a gate attraction—he couldn't hit, field, or pitch. Above all, the game needed something or someone to bring the fans streaming back to the parks as in the years before the Federal League war.

Magically, baseball found the answer to all its ills in the powerful bat of a moon-faced kid from Baltimore, George Herman Ruth.

Babe Ruth, as he came to be known to millions the world over, was born in Baltimore on February 6, 1895, one of eight children. His father owned a cheap barroom, where George was required to do chores. With both his father and mother working long hours, George found plenty of time to get into trouble. He became so uncontrollable that his parents sent him to St. Mary's Industrial School for Boys. He was seven years old when he first entered. By the time he was 19, he had been in and out of the school five times.

St. Mary's was a poor and struggling institution. But life there was good for George in many ways. It brought his wild nature under some degree of control. And it gave him the opportunity of playing baseball on an organized team.

George Ruth's first tutor was Brother Mathias, a considerate, kind man who understood boys and knew how to handle them.

Brother Mathias saw many good qualities in George, although others had branded him an incorrigible. Like almost any boy, George responded to kindness and understanding. He worked hard at learning his trade—that of a shirtmaker. He also worked hard at learning how to play baseball.

George Ruth had another friend at St. Mary's—Brother Gilbert, head of the school. Fortunately for George, Brother Gilbert was friendly with Jack Dunn, owner of the Baltimore Orioles.

When Ruth was 19, Brother Gilbert told Dunn about the boy.

"He's got great potential as a pitcher," Brother Gilbert said. "I wish you'd take a look at him."

One look was enough for Dunn.

"I'll take him," he said.

But since Ruth had been committed to St. Mary's by the courts, Dunn had to agree that he would be responsible for the youth's conduct until he was 21. This he did, and in February of 1914 Ruth, nervous and apprehensive, left St. Mary's for the Orioles' training camp.

When owner Jack Dunn first put a Baltimore uniform on the youngster, one of the Orioles slapped his leg with glee and shouted:

"Look! Here's another one of Dunn's babes!"

In his first intra-squad game, the Babe hit the longest homer ever seen in the Oriole training camp. But it wasn't the home run that impressed his manager. It was the way the rookie could pitch.

Babe Ruth shakes hands with his boss, Colonel Jacob Ruppert, co-owner of the Yankees.

As the Orioles ran through their schedule in the early part of the season, Ruth began to rack up one win after another.

The Orioles were in trouble, though, despite the presence of the bright young rookie. For that was the year the Federal League moved a team into Baltimore. Jack Dunn began to lose money trying to compete. Finally he had no choice but to sell off some of his players. Ruth, Ernie Shore, and Ben Egan went to the Boston Red Sox for less than $10,000.

Ruth hit his first major league home run in the Polo Grounds on May 6, 1915, as a rookie pitcher for the Red Sox. He banged out three more that season. In 1917 he hit but two.

Ruth was not only a good hitter but also one of the best base stealers on the club. Manager Ed Barrow wanted him in the lineup every day. When not pitching, Ruth went to the outfield.

Ruth's hitting, however, didn't begin to draw the attention of the fans until 1919. That year he hit 29 homers, breaking the record of 27 set by Ed Williamson in 1884. Baseball officials were quick to see the effect the home run had on the fans. They gave more life to the ball for the 1920 season.

But Ruth was no longer in a Red Sox uniform when he started the 1920 season. During the winter months Red Sox owner Harry Frazee, badly in debt, offered Ruth to the New York Yankees for $100,000 in cash and a loan of $385,000. The two Colonels—Ruppert and Huston —accepted the offer, and the biggest player transaction in baseball history went through.

Once seen the Ruthian homer was never forgotten.

There was one little hitch before Ruth put on his new uniform. To the delight of fans everywhere, Ruth announced that the Yankees would have to increase his salary.

"Yep," he told the astonished colonels, "you've got to double it."

The colonels swallowed hard, but gave Ruth a contract for $20,000.

For the first two weeks of the season, Ruth looked like a poor investment. He didn't get a single hit. But his sights were adjusted by May 1, when he hit his first homer. By July he had passed his 1919 record of 29. And at the end of the season he had lashed out a staggering total of 54—25 more than his own record and 27 more than any other player in the entire history of the game! In addition, he batted .376 to lead the League.

The fans talked of him endlessly—about his personality, his every move on the diamond. For Ruth was unique in many ways. Although a big man, he stood at the plate with his feet close together, toes turned inward slightly. His body was straight from the waist down. From the waist up, he leaned forward a bit.

From the stands it appeared that Ruth was listening to something that was going on behind him as he waited for the pitch. His head would be cocked to the right and held rock-still.

Ruth used one of the biggest bats in the majors—42 ounces. Nevertheless he held it at the end, which was unusual in his day. As he waited for the pitch, the bat would be pointed skyward, well to the left of his left shoulder. Usually the fat end moved in a slow circle. It re-minded a spectator of the way a cat twitches its tail before pouncing on a mouse.

Once seen, the Ruthian homer was never forgotten. Most home-run hitters power the ball into the seats or over the wall on either a line or a high arc. But Ruth's hits soared lazily skyward to dizzying heights, then carried farther and farther from the plate. When they dropped, they seemed to drop straight down. Even the shots that stayed in the park often amazed the fans. Once Ruth hit a fly to the infield. It went so high that Jimmy Dykes got dizzy circling around beneath it. The ball fell in back of Dykes and, by the time he had recovered it, Ruth was standing on second.

The Yankees, playing at the Polo Grounds, outdrew their landlords, the Giants, by a wide margin. As a matter of fact, they established an attendance record of 1,289,422. It wasn't topped until 26 years later.

Why did the fans flock to wherever the Yankees played? To see Babe Ruth.

The impact the round-faced slugger made on the game is still evident today.

27. A Pennant for the Yankees

Babe Ruth was no ordinary man on the diamond. He was no ordinary man off it, either. Baseball has never known a wilder, more carefree, fun-loving, free-spending, big-hearted player. Neither has it known a player loved by so many, especially by boys and girls.

Ruth burst upon the baseball scene when America seemed bent on living wildly. It was the start of a period known as "The Roaring Twenties." As the 1921 season ran its course, Babe Ruth seemed to set the pace for the topsy-turvy world. He fought openly with pint-sized Miller Huggins, his manager. He consistently broke training. He deliberately ignored front-office rules.

When the team was traveling, for example, the players were assigned hotel rooms that cost about $3 a day. Ruth moved into suites that cost $100 a day. If the team traveled to Boston, or Washington, or Philadelphia by train—Ruth would go by car. Once, as he raced between Philadelphia and Washington, his car overturned on the treacherous roads. Miraculously he escaped with but minor injuries.

Ruth's mode of living didn't seem to affect his playing that year. He hit 59 homers, batted .378 and knocked in 170 runs. He led the League in RBIs and homers. More important, he paced the New York Yankees to their first American League championship.

And what team did the New York Yankees have to face in the 1921 World Series? Dramatically enough, it was an-other New York team—the Giants.

John McGraw, cocky and combative as ever, couldn't wait to get at the Yankees, a team that had stolen his public—and right in his own ball park.

McGraw got his vengeance, too. His proud Giants whipped the upstart Yankees 5–3.

Yankee fans had a ready alibi. Ruth hadn't played in the last three games because of an injury. The Giants hooted at this. One sports writer even went so far as to hint that Ruth was faking. When Ruth read the story, he became so angry he tried to force his way into the press box and attack the writer.

Still smarting from the crushing defeat at the hands of the Giants, Ruth took on another opponent after the Series ended. It was Judge Landis.

In the view of Judge Kenesaw Mountain Landis, the rules of the National Commission, which governed all of professional baseball, were not to be broken by anyone. And that included George Herman Ruth, the biggest sports personality in America.

Ruth had a different opinion. When the 1921 World Series ended, he announced that he and teammates Bob Meusel and Bill Piercy were going on a barnstorming trip. Each man was to receive $1,000 a day. Judge Landis pointed out that the rules forbade players from participating in baseball games once the season closed.

"The heck with the old goat," Ruth said. "I'm not under contract and if I want to play ball, I'll play ball!"

Meusel and Piercy agreed, and the three went ahead with their plans. They were soon to regret it.

Not only did the tour fail after six days, but Judge Landis showed the boys he was not to be trifled with.

He ordered the players' World Series shares, which amounted to about $3,000 each, held back. He also suspended them for the first 40 days of the following season.

Both the Yankee management and Ban Johnson, president of the American League, as well as press and public, were stunned by the severity of the Landis ruling. All of them set up a thunderous howl.

The Yankees and the American League pointed out that Ruth was baseball's biggest attraction. To keep him out of the lineup for a whole month might cost them thousands of dollars.

"He can't do this!" was the cry heard from every side.

Landis stood firm.

With Ruth and Meusel out of uniform, the Yankees floundered badly during the spring. And even after the players rejoined the club, everything went wrong.

Ruth and his mates created most of the trouble themselves. They fought with each other. They refused to obey training rules. In short, they did about

The fun-loving Babe poses with the four-year-old Yankee mascot, little Ray Kelly.

A handshake marks the end of one of Ruth's many feuds with manager Miller Huggins.

everything athletes should *not* do. Ed Barrow, general manager of the Yankees, and Miller Huggins tried mightily to bring the team to its senses. And somehow the New Yorkers finally managed to win their second pennant. They slipped into the 1922 championship one game ahead of Cleveland.

But although they won the pennant, the Yankees failed to capture the big prize, the World Series. And it was the New York Giants, to the utter delight of John McGraw, who kept it from them. The Giants whipped the Yankees in four of five games! (One game ended in a tie.)

As for Ruth, he had the poorest Series record ever. He batted a lowly .118, gaining but two hits in 17 trips to the plate.

The Ruth suspension and the World Series whipping at the hands of the Giants taught the Yankees a much-needed lesson.

28. New Seeds

New names pop into baseball every year. Some disappear quickly. Others remain and become a part of the great legend of the game. While Babe Ruth blazed a new record with his booming homers, a serious, intelligent, and ambitious man named Branch Rickey was moving into the limelight.

Rickey had paid his way through Ohio Wesleyan with earnings from playing football and baseball. He made the majors in 1905, and was purchased by the Cincinnati Reds after two seasons as a catcher at Dallas.

But the Reds got rid of Rickey because he refused to play ball on Sunday. He was signed then by the New York Highlanders and later by the St. Louis Browns.

Branch Rickey was a competent player but not a great one. Soon he became interested in managing—both on the field and in the front office. Before World War I, he managed the Browns. In 1919, he took over as pilot of the St. Louis Cardinals. The Cardinals were a last-place club, badly in debt with little prospect of being able to do anything about it.

During the season the New York Giants became interested in Rogers Hornsby, the only really valuable ball player the Cardinals had under contract. Manager John McGraw and Charles Stoneham, a new Giant owner, paid Rickey a visit.

"We'll give you five Giant players for Hornsby," McGraw said.

Rickey smiled and said nothing.

McGraw then added a sum of cash to the offer.

Rickey still showed no interest.

Soon Stoneham took over the bidding. He offered Rickey the five players and $100,000 for Hornsby. He went to $125,-000, then $150,000. As the bidding went on, McGraw drew up a lineup for Rickey to show him how the five Giant players could be used.

Though Stoneham finally offered $250,000 along with the five players, Rickey was unmoved.

"Rogers Hornsby is the only great ball player I've got and I can't sell him," was Rickey's attitude. The deal fell through.

Rickey soon had occasion to regret his decision—at least temporarily. Hornsby, driving into second on the front end of a double play, was hit on the head by a thrown ball. He had to be carried from the field on a stretcher.

Luckily Hornsby recovered. He went on to become the greatest right-handed batter the game has ever seen, leading his league six straight times. During 22 years in the majors, Hornsby batted over .400 four times. Once he hit .424, the highest average ever attained by a modern player. His lifetime average of .358 is topped only by Ty Cobb.

The shock of seeing Hornsby almost killed by a thrown ball gave Branch Rickey plenty of food for thought. He realized that it was dangerous to bank so heavily on a single player. What he

A thoughtful Rogers Hornsby waits for his turn at bat.

needed was not one Rogers Hornsby, but a dozen.

Since rosters of major league clubs are limited, Rickey conceived the idea of placing players in the minor league teams, where they could be controlled and trained. With the backing of owner Sam Breadon, he began stocking several minor league teams with a great corps of untried rookies.

The Cards, chiefly because of Rickey's foresight, moved from last place in 1919 to a tie for third place in 1922. They then suffered a slump, but later went on to their greatest period of glory.

The year the Cardinals tied for third

place was the same season the Giants humiliated the Yankees in World Series play. It was also the year Rickey saw one of his former players win the American League's Most Valuable Player Award. The player was George Sisler. He had a .420 batting average and 51 stolen bases.

Although hampered by eye trouble, Sisler batted .340 during his 15 years in the majors. He was considered to be almost as good a hitter as Hornsby.

By 1922 the Giants had added many new names to the growing list of stars playing in the majors. Among them was a graduate of Fordham University, Frank Frisch. Frisch, who started at third base, then moved to second, could easily have been included among the tough Orioles of the 1880s. He would have been right at home alongside John McGraw and Hughie Jennings, for he played baseball as though he were playing for his life. He was tough, courageous, and skillful.

About this time the Giants acquired another McGraw type of player—a scrawny, scrappy outfielder who started his adult life as a left-handed dentist. The new outfielder, Charles Dillon Stengel, loved to win ball games. He also delighted McGraw by keeping him company at all hours of the night as he talked about baseball.

Stengel, nicknamed "Casey" because he hailed from Kansas City, warmed the hearts of Giant fans in the 1923 Series against the Yankees. In each of two games, he hit homers to give the Giants a victory. As he circled the bases after hitting the second one, the brash youngster thumbed his nose at the Yankee bench. Little did he realize that some-day he would be sitting on that bench building baseball's greatest managerial record.

The Yankees of 1923, however, were not to be underestimated. They started the year with a different attitude and in a new home, Yankee Stadium.

Babe Ruth, always able to rise to the occasion, christened the stadium in true Ruthian style. With two men on base, he hit a homer, giving the Yankees a 4–2 victory. His home run started them toward their third pennant. In World Series play, the mighty Yanks revenged the crushing defeat of the year before, downing the Giants 4–2. Ruth, who won the homer title with 41, made up for his terrible 1922 showing by crashing out three homers, a triple, double, and three singles. This performance, plus his .393 season average, won him the Most Valuable Player award. He was the first Yankee to earn that distinction.

Although Ruth led the American League home-run parade again in 1924, the Yankees finished second to the Washington Senators. And with the Senators' victory, the name of Stanley Raymond "Bucky" Harris burst into prominence.

Harris, the Senators' second baseman, took over as manager of the team after several others had failed to pull the ball club together. Dubbed "The Boy Wonder," Harris handled the club with great skill, leading it from seventh place to the pennant.

Harris, of course, was blessed with one of the finest pitchers in the game—Walter Johnson. Although past his prime, Johnson worked as never before. In the

A new Giant star, Frank Frisch, who played baseball for all he was worth.

stretch drive as the Senators fought to overtake the Yankees, Johnson won 11 in a row. He finished the season with a 23–7 record.

Washington's opponent in the 1924 World Series was the tough New York Giants. Although Harris realized Johnson was worn out by the pennant fight, he gave the big pitcher the opening-game assignment. Johnson pitched well, but the Senators lost 4 to 3 in 12 innings. Johnson also lost the fifth game 6–2. In the twelfth inning of the seventh game, the score was tied when one of the Senators hit a hot drive. The ball struck a pebble in front of the Giants' third base-man, Freddy Lindstrom, and bounded

The fabulous Waner brothers—Paul and Lloyd.

over his head. That freakish bounce gave the Senators their first World Series.

The following year, Johnson gave his all again, winning 20 and losing 7 as he paced the Senators to still another pennant. This time the Senators met the Pittsburgh Pirates in the Series.

Like the Pirates of 1960, the Pittsburgh club of 1925 was built around youngsters, among them talented Paul Waner. (Lloyd Waner joined Paul in the outfield the next year. So potent were their bats, they were referred to as "Big Poison" and "Little Poison.") Pacing the Pirates' attack was Harold "Pie" Traynor, often rated the game's best third baseman. Traynor batted .320. This was his average for the 17 years he played in the majors.

The Pirate-Washington Series went to seven games—the same number as the year before. But it seemed to have more thrills. Walter Johnson, the sentimental favorite of fans everywhere, won the first and fourth games by scores of 4–1 and 4–0. But he lost the seventh game 9–7. The Senators' Roger Peckinpaugh committed two of his eight Series errors, letting in four runs.

It was Johnson's last World Series and his next-to-last season. In spring training in 1927, a batting-practice line drive broke his ankle, ending his career.

Lou Gehrig impressed everyone with the ferocious way he could hit a baseball.

29. The Iron Horse

On June 2, 1925, the New York Yankees' veteran first baseman, Wally Pipp, had to leave a game because of a headache. He was replaced by a rookie who had played in his first Yankee game the day before. The rookie's name was Henry Louis Gehrig.

Pipp next played first base a year later, and in another league. When Gehrig took over from Pipp, he started a consecutive game-playing streak that in all probability will never be broken. In a span of 14 years, he played in 2,130 consecutive games!

Gehrig, who had played both football and baseball in high school, came from a poor, hard-working family. After Lou graduated from high school, he and his mother and father worked in a fraternity house at Columbia University, where Gehrig had enrolled. Lou waited on table, while his mother cooked and his father did the house maintenance work.

While at Columbia, Gehrig was given a workout at the Polo Grounds under the watchful eye of John McGraw. The big, square-shouldered college boy immediately impressed McGraw with the ferocious way he could hit a baseball.

The wily McGraw sent Gehrig to Hartford, a Class A team in the Eastern League. He told Gehrig to play under the name of "Lewis," so he could protect his amateur standing and remain eligible for sports at Columbia. Columbia officials learned of the trick, however, and quickly persuaded Gehrig to leave Hartford.

The next year, while pitching for Columbia against Rutgers University, Gehrig hit two long home runs. Columbia won by a score of 9–4. A Yankee scout saw the game, raced to a phone, and called the Yankee front office.

"I've found another Ruth!" he cried.

Gehrig signed a contract with the Yankees in 1923. He was then farmed out to Hartford, where he played about a third of the season and hit 24 homers. The next year he went to spring training with the Yankees, but was returned to Hartford where he batted .368 and hit 37 homers. When the Eastern League season closed, Gehrig rejoined the Yankees and there he stayed.

Lou Gehrig, always quiet and dignified, disciplined himself and worked hard at his trade. Even after he became a star, he continued to try to improve and never held himself above correction or instruction.

Like Babe Ruth, Lou Gehrig's feats on the diamond have filled the record books. In each of 13 seasons, he knocked in 100 or more runs. His lifetime average was .340 over a 17-year span. In his total of 2,721 hits, he had 493 homers, 161 triples and 535 doubles. Twenty-three of Gehrig's homers came with the bases loaded. On three occasions he hit three homers in a single game. In one game he hit four in a row.

With Gehrig batting behind Ruth, the Yankees developed the greatest 1–2 punch that baseball has ever known. The two of them paced the Yanks to another pennant in 1926. The World Series, though, was a different matter.

30. End of a Drought

Until 1926, the St. Louis Cardinals had never won a pennant. They weren't expected to win one in 1926 either. But they did.

There were a number of reasons why the Cards were able to take the flag. First, Branch Rickey's chain-store methods began to show results. Secondly, Rogers Hornsby became playing manager of the club.

Hornsby showed that he was as good a manager as player. Like John McGraw he ruled his club with an iron hand. Hornsby did not have an overpowering ball club, but he squeezed every bit of ability from his players. In addition, he made two trades that helped the Cardinals immensely.

One involved Billy Southworth of the Giants. While Southworth seemed just an average ball player under McGraw, he blossomed into a star when switched to the Cardinals.

Hornsby also snatched up Grover Cleveland Alexander, when the Chicago Cubs put the aging pitcher on the waiver list.

Alexander had been in baseball since 1909 and in the big leagues since 1911. In each of six of his first seven years, he won 22 games or more. On three occasions, while pitching for Philadelphia, he won 30 games. Traded to the Cubs, he continued to be a big winner until 1924. By that time the Cubs—like almost everyone else in baseball—were sure Alexander had come to the end of the road.

The Yankees took three of the first five World Series games in 1926. Babe Ruth, as usual, led the attack. In the fourth game he set a Series record by hitting three home runs.

Although the Cardinals trailed, Hornsby showed his faith in Alexander by calling on him to hurl the sixth game. The old pitcher responded beautifully. The Cards won, tying the Series at three-all. Billy Southworth was a big help to Alexander. He collected a double and a triple. At one point, with two Yankees on base, he made a diving, head-first catch of a sizzling line drive.

After the game, Alexander celebrated, certain he wouldn't be called to duty in the final game. Hornsby, however, decided to have him in the bullpen "just in case."

The Cards were leading the Yanks by a slim margin in the seventh inning of the seventh game, and it looked as if St. Louis would win its first World Championship. Then suddenly pitcher Jess Haines seemed to lose all control of the ball. After getting two strikes on Lou Gehrig, he floated four bad pitches to the plate. Then two more Yankees walked.

"Time out!" Hornsby yelled at the umpires.

Hornsby and the rest of the Cardinal infield gathered around Haines and quickly discovered what was wrong. Haines had thrown so many knuckle balls he had injured the index finger of his pitching hand.

"We'll have to make a change," Hornsby said grimly, for he knew that

85

one of the Yankees' toughest hitters—
Tony Lazzeri—was waiting at the plate.

As Haines took off his glove and moved
dejectedly toward the Cardinal dugout, Hornsby, to everyone's amazement,
waved in Grover Alexander.

The aging pitcher shuffled slowly out
onto the playing field. His cap was
perched on one side of his head, and his
jaws moved slowly over a cud of tobacco.
Every eye in the ball park turned toward
him.

To the fans, Alexander seemed dazed.
Actually he was thinking carefully about
the situation he faced—the inning, the
score, and the batter.

As the fans buzzed, a worried Hornsby
trotted out to meet his pitcher. Later,
Hornsby reported that he knew Alexander was all right as soon as he got a
good look at him.

Methodically Alexander took his warm-
up tosses. Then he faced Lazzeri. The
first pitch was low. "Ball one!" The second was a strike. On the next pitch,
Lazzeri swung. Crack! The ball whizzed
into the left-field seats.

"Foul ball!" cried the umpire. It was
foul, but just by inches. Alexander and
every Cardinal rooter and player in the
park sighed in relief.

The pitcher fussed about the mound
a bit, looked at his catcher's sign, then
fired again.

"Strike thu-ree!"

The ball park rocked with cheers. The
Cardinal bench teemed with excitement.
But Alexander moved to a quiet corner
of the dugout, ignoring everyone.

When a worried teammate questioned
him, Alexander said:

*In the seventh inning of the seventh 1926
Series game, Cardinal pitcher Grover Cleveland Alexander (above) faced one of the
Yankees' toughest hitters, Tony Lazzeri (below).*

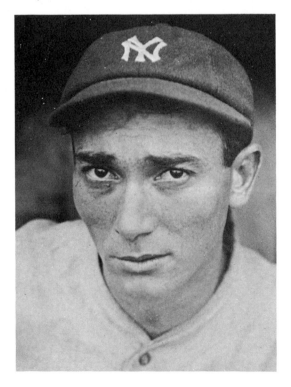

"Oh, I'm all right. I was just thinking that if I get the side out in the eighth, I'll have a chance to strike Ruth out for the final out."

Alexander set the Yankees down in order in the eighth inning. He also got the first two men out in the ninth. Then Babe Ruth stepped to the plate. By that time he had collected *four* home runs. He had also broken 10 World Series records.

As every fan knew, Ruth could change the whole complexion of the game with one swish of his bat. Naturally Alexander pitched slowly and carefully.

Ball one. Strike one. Ball two. Strike two. Ball three.

Alexander wound and fired the full-count pitch.

"Ball four!" the umpire roared as Alexander missed the corner of the plate. The great Ruth trotted to first base. On Alexander's next pitch, he broke for second. The catcher fired to Hornsby. An umpire's hand shot skyward. His "Yer out!" call was drowned in the roar of the crowd.

The Series was over. The Cardinals became World Champions for the first time in baseball history.

31. The Mightiest Team of All

It's easy to start an argument among ball fans. All you need do, for example, is tell a Giant follower that Connie Mack was a far better manager than John Mc-Graw. Or that Mickey Mantle can run rings around Willie Mays.

You can get some mighty sharp retorts, too, when trying to name the greatest ball team of all time. Unless, that is, you happen to name the New York Yankees of 1927. For this was a team that had everything—speed, crushing power, and a marvelous defense.

The 1927 Yankees started the season in first place—and finished in first place. The winning margin? Nineteen games. The number of victories? One hundred and ten, at that time an American League record.

Babe Ruth, prodded to tremendous efforts by Lou Gehrig, the rookie at first base, stirred fans as never before. For that was the year the home-run king smashed out a total of 60 home runs. Only a few have come close to that record in a 154-game season.

With but one month of the season left, the Bambino had already lofted the ball out of the park 43 times. During that last month—with every fan in the nation watching the results and wondering just how far the big fellow could go—he hit 17, a little better than one every two days.

With two days left, the Babe's total was 57. On the next to last day, he hit two more. Number 60 was blasted into the seats during the final game of the season. The drive itself had a touch of drama. It landed in fair ground by no more than a foot!

Gehrig hit an additional 47 homers, 13 short of Ruth's total. He drove in 174 runs to Ruth's 164, however, while his batting average was .373 to Ruth's .356. He also led the League in doubles.

But Ruth and Gehrig didn't do all the hitting for the Yankees. Center fielder Earle Combs batted .356 and led the League in singles. Left fielder Bob Meusel batted .336. Second baseman Tony Lazzeri pounded out 18 homers and batted .309.

So fearsome was the hitting of this group that it became known as "Murderer's Row." Only one pitcher, Bob Grove of the Athletics, was able to hold the Yankees scoreless in 1927. In a tingling ball game, the A's won 1–0.

Baseball teams do not win pennants without good pitching. The Yankees of 1927 certainly had their share of it. Pitcher Waite Hoyt won 22 games, while losing 7. Herb Pennock won another 19. Much of the credit for the performance of the mound staff, however, went to a relief pitcher—Wilcy "Cy" Moore. This "fireman" appeared in 50 games. He won 19 and lost but 7.

Despite this great performance, the baseball experts felt the Yankees would have trouble in the 1927 World Series. Their opponents were the Pittsburgh Pirates, paced by Paul Waner and Pie Traynor. (Waner hit .380, the best in the National League, while Traynor drove in 124 runs.)

The Pittsburgh club had never fielded a better team.

Before the Series opened in Pittsburgh, both teams worked out in Forbes Field. The Bucs were on the diamond first. Then they dressed and sat in the stands to watch the Yanks, a team most of them had never seen.

To the astonishment and awe of the Pirates, the Yanks seemed to hit only homers during batting practice. The Pirates didn't know it, but sly Miller Huggins had ordered his pitchers to lay the ball in the strike zone without much speed.

Despite a popular legend, the batting practice bombardment didn't faze the Bucs. They fought hard against the Yankees.

The Yanks won the first game 5–4, but three runs were unearned. Ruth failed to hit a homer, although Gehrig hit a triple.

In the second game, the Yanks won 6–2, but the big gun—Babe Ruth—was almost silent in the 11-hit attack.

Unfortunately for the Pirates, Herb Pennock was at his best in the third game at Yankee Stadium. He retired the first 22 batters to face him. It was still a close ball game, though, until the seventh inning. Finally Ruth broke loose, rocketing a drive into the seats with two on base, thereby topping a six-run rally. The final score: Yankees 8, Pittsburgh 1.

The Pirates fought gamely in the fourth contest to prevent a sweep of the Series. Early in the game, Ruth singled one run home. In the fifth inning, he hit a homer with one on base, giving the Yanks a 3 to 0 lead. But the Pirates stormed back in the seventh to tie the score.

The Babe is congratulated by Lou Gehrig at home plate after smashing out his sixtieth homer.

The New York Yankees of 1927. (Bottom row left to right) Ruether, Dugan, Paschal, Bengough, Thomas, Gazella, Morehart, and Eddie Bennett, mascot. (Middle row) Shawkey, Giard, Grabowski, O'Leary, Manager Huggins, Fletcher, Pennock, Wera, Collins. (Top row) Gehrig, Meusel, Ruth, Moore, Pipgras, Combs, Miller, Hoyt, Lazzeri, Koenig, Shocker, Durst, and Doc Woods, trainer.

With the score still tied in the bottom of the ninth, the Yankees quickly loaded the bases. But Pirate pitcher John Miljus struck out Gehrig, then Meusel. A wild pitch to the next batter, however, struck the catcher on the knee and bounded into the infield. The break let in the winning run and gave the New York team its second World Series championship.

The Yankees were almost as impressive in 1928. Again they won the pennant, with Ruth hitting 54 homers. And again they crushed the opposition—the St. Louis Cardinals—in the World Series by taking the first four games. Ruth was superb. He gathered 10 hits in 16 appearances for a .625 average. Three of his hits were homers.

It's hard to believe there was ever a better baseball team than the Yankees of 1927 and 1928.

32. Revival in Philadelphia

Was Connie Mack through as a manager? Had he lost his great ability to judge talent and pilot winners? There were many who thought so when the season started in 1929. After all, the Athletics hadn't won a pennant since 1914.

Mack, of course, heard the grumbling, but he paid no attention. As the New York Yankees went roaring through the American League, he slowly rebuilt his once powerful Philadelphia team. He dipped into the Pacific Coast League to sign black-haired, big-eared Mickey Cochrane, a catcher batting .331. He went to Milwaukee and landed Al Simmons, an outfielder batting .398. His old third baseman, Home Run Baker, brought him a 17-year-old giant named Jimmy Foxx. He also brought Robert Moses "Lefty" Grove from Baltimore for $100,000 after the big pitcher had struck out 1,020 batters over a four-year period.

The four were not polished performers when they arrived in Philadelphia, but each had the mark of greatness. They developed rapidly. To this day, Mickey Cochrane is rated as one of the best catchers baseball ever produced. As a slugger, Jimmy Foxx ranks second only to Babe Ruth. Al Simmons knew no peer whenever he stood at the plate with runners on base. As for Grove, he led the American League four times and is one of 13 pitchers who won 300 or more games in the majors.

With this quartet as the nucleus of his ball club, Mack rode to a sixth pennant in 1929. His National League opponent for the World Championship was a soft-spoken, black-eyed Irishman of few words—Joe McCarthy, pilot of the Chicago Cubs.

McCarthy, Mack knew, was a smart manager. He had taken over the Cubs in 1926, after they had spent a season at the bottom of the League. And he had

Catcher Mickey Cochrane (above) and pitcher Lefty Grove (below) were two of the Athletics' stars who helped bring about a "revival in Philadelphia." (In 1934 Grove moved to Boston.)

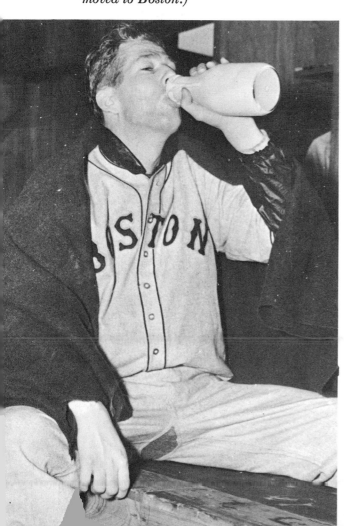

forged the team into a pennant winner. In his lineup he had the powerful bats of Rogers Hornsby (formerly of the Cardinals), Hack Wilson, and a tomato-faced catcher affectionately known as "Gabby" Hartnett.

Before the season ended, it became fairly obvious that the Cubs and A's would win the flag in their respective leagues. So Mack planned his strategy long before the World Series opener. He revealed these plans to but one man—pitcher Howard Ehmke. To Ehmke's utter surprise, Mack told him:

"Howard, you're going to pitch the first game against the Cubs for me."

"But the season won't be over for another week, or more," Ehmke commented.

"I know," Mack said. "But while we're making our last western trip, the Cubs will be playing New York and Philadelphia on their eastern swing. I want you to stay behind and scout them."

And that's what Ehmke did.

When the first day of the World Series arrived, Ehmke's name was announced as the A's starter. Against him was the Cubs' tough Charlie Root. Groans of disbelief rolled through the Philadelphia rooters.

"Is Mack daft?" some asked. "Why Ehmke's an old man. He's won only seven games all season. Why doesn't Mack start Grove or Earnshaw?"

But Mack wasn't daft, as Ehmke proved. The aging pitcher held the Cubs scoreless until the ninth inning when a run came in on a two-base error. It didn't matter, though, for young Jimmy Foxx had cracked the ball into the

91

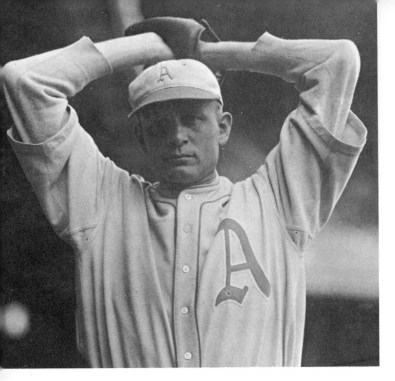

On the first day of the 1929 Series, pitcher Howard Ehmke's name was announced as starter for the Athletics.

bleachers for a run in the seventh inning, while his mates added two more in the ninth. The A's won 3–1. And Ehmke established a new World Series record by striking out 13.

After that stirring start, the A's were almost invincible. They won the series in five games, handing Mack his fourth World Championship, one more than John McGraw's and Miller Huggins' teams had won.

In 1929 the United States began to feel the pinch of the worst depression in its history. Like the rest of the entertainment business, baseball was hard hit.

The worried owners decided that the fans were staying away from the parks because they were tired of seeing so many home runs. So they deadened the ball to encourage the hit-and-run, steal, and bunt techniques.

This change didn't bother the Athletics. In 1930 they won their second straight pennant and whipped the up-and-coming St. Louis Cardinals in six games of World Series play.

The following year Lefty Grove, the dour, hard-bitten mountaineer, had his best season with 31 victories and 4 losses. The Athletics won their third consecutive pennant. The Cardinals, too, won the pennant in 1931. But because of one man, the World Series did not end as it had the year before.

33. Pepper

The St. Louis Cardinals had a talented outfielder-infielder who seemed to have the combined spirit and fire of John McGraw, Hughie Jennings, and Ty Cobb. His name was John "Pepper" Martin.

Frolicsome and happy-go-lucky, Martin enjoyed playing practical jokes on people almost as much as he loved playing baseball. He was especially fond of handing out loaded cigars and cigarettes. Once he leaned out of a hotel window and dropped a paper bag filled with water on the head of his manager.

The enraged manager raced through the hotel until he caught Martin.

"It slipped, honest," Martin grinned.

"If you'll forgive me, I'll hit a homer in the next game."

The manager gave Martin a shake and let him go. The next day the third baseman kept his promise. His home run won the ball game.

Although Martin was a good ball player, few believed he would have more than a routine role in the 1931 World Series against the Athletics. During the first game, Martin got three hits off Lefty Grove, but the A's won anyhow. So the fans were unaware of what was in store for them. In the second game, however, they began to get an inkling of the surprises awaiting them.

In his first time at bat, Martin singled. As the Philadelphia outfielder bobbled the ball momentarily, Martin flew to second and dived into the bag. The outfielder's throw arrived at about the same time. Martin, however, was safe by a whisker.

The fans had barely settled back in their seats when Martin did what many considered impossible. He stole third against Mickey Cochrane! A fly ball then brought him home.

John "Pepper" Martin

In the seventh inning, Martin singled a second time. To show that his first theft of a base wasn't just luck, he promptly swiped the keystone sack. When the next batter hit the ball to the shortstop, Martin broke all the rules of good base running by racing to third on the infield play.

As the pitcher wound up and fired to the next hitter Martin was off for the plate. At the last instant, the batter bunted the ball. The squeeze play worked beautifully and Martin slid home with the second run of the game.

St. Louis won that second game and tied the Series. In the important third game, Martin put on another show. In the second inning, he singled a man to third, then went to third on a hit-and-run play, and scored on a fly ball.

In the fourth inning, with a man on first, Martin bought the crowd roaring to its feet when he hit a drive to the top of the right-field scoreboard. A few feet more and the ball would have cleared the wall for a homer. Instead, it dropped to the field. Martin was held to a double, while his teammate stopped at third. Another hit drove in both runs and the Cards went on to win 5–2. This gave them a 2 to 1 lead in the Series.

The Athletics, with veteran George Earnshaw on the mound, won the fourth game 3–0, tying the Series again. Earnshaw seemed able to get everyone out—everyone but Martin. The amazing Cardinal third sacker got two hits and rattled Cochrane again by stealing still another base.

Martin rose to even greater heights in the fifth game. With three hits—one of them a homer—he drove in four of the Cardinals' five runs.

St. Louis lost the sixth game, but won the deciding seventh. Appropriately Martin made a sparkling, one-hand catch for the last out.

Rarely has one man put on such a show in a World Series.

34. The "Called" Shot

Was Babe Ruth a miracle man? Could he call on some superhuman power and hit a homer whenever it was especially important?

Many would dismiss these questions as being too ridiculous to consider. Others are not so sure. They are thinking, no doubt, of Ruth's role in the 1932 World Series.

That season the Babe's home-run production had dropped to 41. But he batted a respectable .341 and drove in 137 runs. Johnny Allen was the Yanks' leading pitcher with 17 victories and 4 losses. As a team, the Yankees were as potent as ever, winning 107 games.

The National League winner was the Chicago Cubs, a team that boasted a new pitching star, Lon Warneke.

The Series opened in New York, and the Yanks promptly won the first two games. By the time the teams arrived in Chicago for the third game, the Cub players were in a bitter frame of mind. They were determined that the Yanks should not repeat their World Series sweeps of 1927 and 1928.

The fans were not so sure. During batting practice Ruth and Gehrig put on an amazing show, pounding 16 homers into the temporary bleachers in deepest center field. Ruth's first blow soared so far and high it almost left the park.

"Each time the ball dropped into the densely packed stands, the crowd gasped," wrote one newspaper reporter. "The spectacle could not have been very heartening to the Cubs."

In the very first inning, Ruth proved his mighty bat was as potent during the game as it was in batting practice. To begin with, the Yanks' Earle Combs had driven a ball right at shortstop Billy Jurges. Jurges, instead of getting an easy out, fired the ball over first baseman Charlie Grimm's head and Combs went to second. This upset pitcher Charley Root, who walked the next man.

Babe Ruth then came to bat. The Cub fans hurled bright yellow lemons at the round-faced slugger, all the while hooting derisively. At the same time, every man in the Cub dugout was on his feet shouting abuse at the Bambino. (The New York *Herald Tribune* later reported that Ruth "paused to jest with the raging Cubs, pointed to the right field bleachers, and grinned.")

Root's first two pitches were wide. Ruth knew the Chicago hurler would

Charlie Root, the man who pitched Ruth's famous "called" shot.

have to get the next one in the strike zone, or risk loading the bases for the next hitter—Lou Gehrig. When the pitch came, Ruth was ready.

"Crack!"

Just as in batting practice, the ball spun over the fence and into the bleachers. The Yanks led 3–0.

The crowd got back at Ruth in the fourth inning when the Cubs were at bat. By that time the score was 4–3, still in favor of the Yanks. Billy Jurges drove a low liner toward Ruth, who raced in and made an attempt to catch the ball at his shoe tops. He missed. Jurges rounded first and sped on. Although Ruth made a fine recovery of the ball and a powerful, accurate throw, Jurges slid into second safely, beating the tag by an eyelash. The Chicago supporters were wild with glee.

Again Ruth seemed to enjoy the storm. He smilingly raised his cap and waved it at the stands. A few minutes later, the fans had another go at him as Tony Lazzeri made an error that enabled Jurges to score the tying run.

The whooping rose to a deafening crescendo in the top of the fifth, for Ruth was the first batter up for the Yankees. As he strode smilingly to the plate, his powerful arms swung three bats from one shoulder to another. He threw two bats to the bat boy and moved into the batter's box. At that moment, a single lemon, glinting brightly in the sunlight, bounded and rolled toward his feet.

With that taunting note, the stage was set for one of the most talked-about scenes in all baseball history.

". . . in no mistaken motion," the New York *Times* later reported, "the Babe notified the crowd that the nature of his retaliation would be a wallop right out of the confines of the park."

The crowd and the Cub bench, apparently galled by Ruth's audacity, heaped new abuse on the Yankee outfielder. Never had such wild-eyed partisanship been witnessed at a World Series.

Charlie Root took his windup, kicked, and whipped the ball past Ruth's knees for a called strike. The shriek of the Chi-

cago rooters hit another high.

Ruth, undisturbed, raised one finger. Grinning broadly, he bobbed his head and waved his hand to the Cub bench and each section of the park. Root pitched again. This time it was "Ball one!"

Ruth, still smiling broadly, again made the appropriate sign with his fingers—one-and-one.

Root kept pitching. The count rose to two-and-two while Ruth continued his pantomime. With each gesture the fans roared anew; some with applause, some with derision.

Root made his fifth pitch. Here's the way a *Times* man described what happened in that memorable moment:

"Then the mightiest blow of all fell. It was a tremendous smash that bore straight over the center in an enormous arc, came down alongside the flagpole and disappeared.

"The crowd, unmindful of anything except that it had just witnessed an epic feat, let loose with a great salvo of applause."

Brought to its feet by Ruth's powerful drive, the crowd had barely settled back when Lou Gehrig lashed another homer to the same spot to drive Charlie Root from the game.

"It was like a flash of lightning and a clap of thunder," a newsman wrote.

The savage blows by Ruth and Gehrig fashioned another victory for the Yankees. In the clubhouse after the game, Ruth modestly brushed aside the praise.

"Shucks, that big wind blowing toward the outfield helped me a lot," he said.

Ruth's home run in the fifth inning of the 1932 World Series has probably created more discussion than any other single play in baseball. Many fans stated that when Ruth raised his hand between the deliveries offered by Root he was telling everybody he intended to blast the ball into the bleachers. In other words, he was "calling the shot."

Root, among others, said Babe did no such thing. He was putting up his finger simply to indicate the count.

For years several writers who attended the game tried to prove that Ruth actually put the ball where he wanted it in the 1932 Series.

Only Ruth really knew.

The big black number "3" meant just one thing to Yankee fans during the 1920s—Babe Ruth.

35. The Loud One

Jay Hanna Dean was a friendly, loud-talking pitcher who made extraordinary claims about what he could do, then went ahead and proved he could do them.

The St. Louis Cardinals signed "Dizzy" Dean in 1929, after he had served a hitch in the Army.

Assigned to St. Joseph of the Western Association, Dean won 17 games in his first season of professional ball. Promoted to Houston of the Texas League, Dean won 26 games.

The next stop, of course, was the parent team, the St. Louis Cardinals. Dean's blazing fast ball and crackling curve enabled him to lead the League in strikeouts four years in a row. And during that period the powerful right-hander struck out more than 200 batters a season.

By the spring of 1934 there were two Deans on the Cardinal roster—Dizzy and his brother, Paul Dean, who later was nicknamed "Daffy."

Although the Cards had finished fifth in 1933, Dizzy freely predicted the Red Birds would easily win the flag in 1934.

"Why, me and Paul will win 40 or 45 games between us," Dizzy said. "If all those other pitchers win mebbe 50 more we'll be in."

The Loud One, surprisingly enough, was too modest in his forecast. The Deans won 49 games.

It wasn't easy, of course. The Dean boys caused all sorts of trouble. After losing a double-header against the Chi-cago Cubs, the Deans deliberately missed a train for Detroit, where the Cardinals were to play the Tigers in an exhibition game. The Cards' new manager, Frank Frisch, promptly slapped a healthy fine on the brothers. Dizzy and Daffy were so enraged they tore up their uniforms. As a matter of fact, they tore them up twice. There weren't any newspaper photographers around to take pictures the first time.

The rest of Frankie Frisch's "Gas House Gang," as the rough-and-tumble Cardinals were called, stood by their manager. So did Commissioner Kenesaw Mountain Landis.

When the Deans saw that they were standing alone, they decided to behave. Their decision was a good thing for the Cards—and for baseball. For the Deans not only won ball games, they also drew fans.

After the Detroit incident, the St. Louis Cardinals won seven in a row and moved into contention for the flag.

It was a tough fight, though. On June 8, 1934, the Giants were in first place. They were still there on September 7, with the Cardinals trailing by seven games. Gradually, however, the Giants lost their lead. On the last day of the season, the Cards were playing Cincinnati while the Giants were host to the Dodgers. The Cards were leading the Giants by one game.

In the ninth inning of their game with the Cincinnati Reds, the Cardinals were ahead 9–0. Dean was on the way to his

The antics of the Dean brothers won them the nicknames of Dizzy (left) and Daffy. Here they are shown in a more sober moment.

thirtieth victory and seventh shutout of the season—the best record in the League. But the pesky Reds suddenly turned on Dean. A single, double, and walk filled the bases with none out.

At this precise moment a message was flashed to the ball park from New York. It read: "Dodgers 8, Giants 5."

A big grin spread across Dizzy's amiable face. He promptly struck out the next two hitters. The third one popped up to the catcher. The Cardinals were National League champions.

The Deans were such an attraction that newspapers often ran headlines like DEANS VS GIANTS TODAY.

The Detroit Tigers had slipped badly after the heyday of their biggest star, Ty Cobb. But Mickey Cochrane, purchased from the Athletics, became manager of the Tigers. And in 1934 he led them to the capture of the American League pennant. Cochrane was blessed with a fine pitching staff that year. A big right-hander, Lynwood Thomas Rowe, was the anchor man of the staff. He won 24 games, while losing only 8. Rowe, familiarly known as "Schoolboy," won 16 of the games in a row.

Tommy Bridges added 22 victories to Rowe's 24 and Eldon Auker won another 15.

Along with good pitching, the Tigers had good hitting—especially from their young first baseman, Henry Benjamin Greenberg. Greenberg, a dedicated player who took his work very seriously, went on to become one of the great batting stars of the game. (Once during his career, he hit nothing but home runs

Pitcher Lynwood "Schoolboy" Rowe (above) and first baseman Hank Greenberg (below) helped the Tigers win the 1934 pennant.

every time he came to bat in nine consecutive games.)

By the opening of the 1934 World Series, Dizzy Dean was telling all who would listen that he and Paul should pitch all the games.

"After all, we won the pennant and we should get the chance to win the Series," Dean said.

The Cardinals won the Series in seven games. Dizzy and Daffy were not allowed to pitch all seven, but they each won two.

Schoolboy Rowe turned in one of the best World Series performances of all time when he retired 22 St. Louis batters in a row in the second game. He made history of another sort when he said a few words to a radio audience, a novelty at that time.

"How'm I doin', Edna?" he said happily. It was a question intended for his fiancée.

After that the brash Cardinals constantly uttered the cry every time Rowe moved about the diamond.

"How'm I doin', Edna? How'm I doin', Edna?" Small wonder that the Cardinals won the final game by a score of 11–0.

36. The Lean One

Most pitchers make a baseball curve by rotating the throwing hand and wrist outward at the end of the delivery. But Carl Owen Hubbell, a left-hander, made a specialty of turning his pitching hand inward as he let go of the ball. This gave him a curving pitch called a "screwball." While the pitch was not entirely new, Hubbell put it to use as never before.

Hubbell had come out of the Texas League to join the Giants in 1928. By the time he left the majors, he had won a total of 253 games. He enjoyed many other distinctions. One season, for example, he pitched 10 shutouts. He also hurled 46 consecutive scoreless innings. He was so reliable a pitcher that the Giants dubbed him "The Meal Ticket."

Hubbell had a long and distinguished career, but he is remembered most for a performance that took place in the Polo Grounds in 1934 before some 50,000 fans. It happened during the first three innings of the second All-Star game.

The tradition of the All-Star game had been introduced in 1933. Arch Ward, sports editor of the Chicago *Tribune*, suggested that a game between the best players of each major league would help build up attendance. It had been slipping badly. Ward also thought the first All-Star game should be played in Chicago, because the World's Fair was opening there that year.

John McGraw, who had recently resigned as manager of the Giants, was selected to manage the National League squad. The leader of the American League team was the ageless Connie Mack. A homer by Babe Ruth paced the

By consecutively striking out five of baseball's most powerful hitters, Carl Hubbell became the talk of the baseball world.

American League to a 4–2 victory.

The second All-Star game was held in New York City in 1934. Just before the start of the game Carl Hubbell was presented with an award naming him as the outstanding National League player of the previous year. But Hubbell didn't look very outstanding as he began his three-inning stint. The first man up, Charlie Gehringer, singled. When outfielder Wally Berger juggled the ball, Gehringer flew to second, sliding safely to the bag just ahead of Berger's throw.

Hubbell, somewhat flustered, then did an unusual thing. He walked the next batter, Heinie Manush. That put two men on base with none out.

The next batter? It was a familiar figure in a Yankee uniform. A big, black Number 3 on back of the player's shirt spelled out his name to all: Babe Ruth.

Hubbell, working slowly and deliberately, went to his "stretch" position, glanced at the runners on first and second, then fired at the plate.

"Ball one!" the umpire yelled.

Hubbell tightened his belt, tugged his cap, and pitched again.

"Strike one!" the umpire tolled, as Ruth watched Hubbell's second pitch go by. The count went on:

"Strike two!"

"Strike thu-reee!"

The Babe turned and walked to the bench. He hadn't even attempted a swing.

Hubbell had a long way to go, though. Behind Ruth was Lou Gehrig. Then Jimmy Foxx, Al Simmons, and Joe Cronin.

Hubbell, seemingly the calmest person in the park, threw Gehrig a ball on the first pitch. He threw three more pitches. All were strikes. Gehringer and Manush worked a double steal as the last pitch whizzed by Gehrig.

Jimmy Foxx came to the plate. A sin-

Jimmy Foxx (left) and Joe Cronin, two of the great hitters struck out by Hubbell in the 1934 All-Star game.

gle would mean two runs. Hubbell remained calm. His first pitch was a strike.

Hubbell glanced at the runner on third, wound up and delivered his second pitch to Foxx. The Athletic slugger took a vicious cut at the ball, but fouled it off. It was strike two.

Carl Hubbell then cut loose with his famous screwball. Foxx went down swinging. The inning was over.

Frank Frisch was the first man up for the National Leaguers. He got his team off to a fast start by banging a homer off the pitch of Vernon "Lefty" Gomez. But Gomez then struck out the next three hitters.

The spotlight swung back to Hubbell. He took up where he had left off in the previous inning. He struck out Al Simmons and Joe Cronin. Bill Dickey, however, made a single, bringing Gomez to

bat. Hubbell threw one pitch. It was a strike. He threw another. Another strike. In swinging at the ball, Gomez' bat slipped from his hand and flew toward second base.

"Leave it there," Frisch yelled at Gomez. "You won't need it."

He was right. Hubbell struck Gomez out on the next pitch.

That finished Hubbell's share of the mound chores. Although the American League eventually won the ball game, Hubbell was the talk of the baseball world. After all, he had consecutively struck out five of baseball's most powerful hitters. And of the fifteen strikes he pitched past these batters, only one—the foul by Foxx—was touched by a bat.

"Unquestionably, it was the greatest pitching performance I have ever seen," Joe Cronin said after the ball game. Few would dispute Cronin's view.

37. From Daylight to Dark

Because of the Great Depression, Americans watched their pocketbooks very carefully in the mid-thirties. Baseball suffered and the club owners looked for ways to bolster the gate receipts. One man in particular favored a new idea— night baseball.

Larry MacPhail was a brilliant, red-haired promoter with a quick temper. He had been hired by a Cincinnati bank to get the ailing Cincinnati Reds on the profit side of the ledger. His proposal to

play baseball under a set of lights horrified both leagues. It also made some of the fans unhappy.

The idea, of course, was not original with MacPhail. Sports contests under lights had been attempted as early as the 1800s. But the lighting equipment was very poor, and the early experiments failed.

Since that time, however, the equipment had improved immensely. So much so that the minor leagues had begun to play night games in 1930. In no time, the minors tripled gate attendance.

"At least let us give it a try," Mac-Phail argued.

Finally the National League agreed. In 1935 the Reds planned seven home games under lights.

MacPhail, always a great showman, staged a fireworks display before the first of the night games. He also cleverly arranged for the President of the United States, Franklin D. Roosevelt, to turn on the lights. The President did this by pressing a button in his office at the White House.

Although the Cincinnati players were enthusiastic about defeating the Philadelphia Phillies that night, they had mixed feelings about playing after dark. Opinion seemed to be divided among the fans, too.

Gradually, however, MacPhail's idea took hold and night baseball became a great success.

38. The Babe Bows Out

Like the Cincinnati Reds, the Boston Braves were also seeking ways to bring fans to their ball park in 1935. Instead of introducing night ball, though, the Braves simply hired the biggest attraction baseball had ever known—Babe Ruth.

The Braves did it in a big way, too. They made Babe a vice-president—the only vice-president who ever played right field.

Although Ruth appeared in but 28 games, he got the usual thundering ovation whenever he moved across the diamond. Of the thirteen hits Babe recorded that year, six were homers.

Three of his homers were among the most memorable of all. He hit them in a game against the Pirates at Forbes Field. And each one had the true Ruthian touch—high, booming arcs that made the fans gasp. One cleared the right-field

roof at Forbes Field, which has rarely been done. That last homer was number 714, a record that stands alone by a wide margin.

But the Babe didn't like being a vaudeville attraction. He was a ball player. And if he couldn't play every day he didn't want to play at all. The season was less than half over when he quietly left the Braves. He was 40 at the time.

Although Babe was ignored for the next three years, he wasn't quite through with baseball. In 1938 he walked into Ebbets Field to watch the Brooklyn Dodgers play. As Ruth's well-known camel-hair cap bobbed along the aisles, the crowd began to murmur. The murmur grew and grew until it was a full-throated roar.

"It's the Babe!" "It's the Babe!" the fans shouted gleefully as they strained to catch a glimpse of the famous player.

Babe Ruth appears at Yankee Stadium in a 1942 benefit game.

The Dodger management got the message fast: there was still magic in the name of Babe Ruth. They hired the Bambino the next day as a batting instructor. It was understood that he would be considered for the manager's job the next year. Although the Dodgers finished seventh, they did very well at the gate. But the Dodgers and the Babe parted company at the end of the season.

The Babe then sought the one thing he wanted most—to manage the New York Yankees. The chance never came. It almost broke his heart.

In August of 1942 he agreed to appear at a benefit game in Yankee Stadium. A smart publicist had dreamed up the idea of having Walter Johnson pitch to the once mighty Ruth during a double-header intermission.

Ruth was 47 at the time, Johnson 55. Ruth hadn't touched a bat in four years, while Johnson hadn't thrown a ball in three. Could Johnson get the ball over the plate? Could Ruth hit it if he did?

Two days before the exhibition Ruth showed he still had some of the old touch. After battling his way through a swarm of youngsters, he took batting practice with the Yanks. With little difficulty he pounded the ball into the seats several times.

On the day Ruth was to face Johnson, the Yankee ball park was opened at 8:30 A.M. By noon more than 69,000 fans filled all available space. And when the first game was over, there was little doubt as to why they had come.

"We want Babe!" "We want Babe!" "We want Babe!" they chanted over and over.

Soon Johnson was taking his famous windup. Ruth, his oval face beaming, stood at the plate as always—feet together, head cocked sideways, bat twitching.

The first pitch by Johnson was a ball. The second a called strike. The third another ball. Then, *bang!* The ball flew into the right-field bleachers for a homer.

"Atta boy, Babe!" the crowd yelled.

Johnson made 15 more pitches. Out of that assortment, Ruth hit a single, high fly, and just missed putting the ball into the bleachers in deepest center field, which would have been a spectacular shot. On the last pitch, Babe powdered the ball deep into the right-field stands. Although it was foul by a few inches, Ruth trotted around the bases, doffing his cap as he went. As he crossed the plate, a grinning Johnson gripped his hand warmly. And after one last, lingering look around the great stadium, Ruth ducked into the dugout and disappeared. The crowd called and called for him to return, but he never did.

It was Ruth's last big scene.

39. The Rookies

Only a few of the hundreds of young men who break into professional baseball each year ever become stars. During the thirties and forties there were four, however, who were so outstanding they will be remembered by ball fans as long as baseball exists.

One of these is the quiet, long-legged Californian who almost replaced Babe Ruth in the hearts of Yankee rooters. His name is Joseph DiMaggio.

Strangely enough, Joe DiMaggio wasn't much interested in baseball as a youngster. He favored tennis. And when he left high school, he went to work to help the family.

But Joe's brothers—Vincent and Dominic—were baseball-minded, and both eventually made their way into the major leagues. They urged young Joe to attend a school for baseball prospects in San Francisco early in the thirties. Spotted by a scout, he was signed by the San Francisco Seals as a shortstop in 1933.

But the Seals already had a veteran shortstop, Augie Galan, and Joe rode the bench for several games. One day, he went into a game to pinch hit. As the inning ended, he thought he was through for the day and headed for the club house. But his manager called out, "Joe, go to right field."

DiMaggio thought the manager was joking and continued to the club house. But his brother Vince, who was also playing the outfield for the Seals, came running after Joe.

"Hey, he means it," Vince said.

"But I never played the outfield in my life," Joe protested.

"You're going to play it now," brother Vince responded.

DiMaggio did and soon set the Pacific Coast League afire, hitting safely at least once in each of 61 consecutive games. In 1935 he batted .398, hit 34 homers, stole 24 bases, and drove in 154 runs.

Although DiMaggio injured his knee in a freak accident, the Yankees gave the Seals $25,000 and five players for the outfielder.

In 1936 DiMaggio opened the season in center field for the Yankees. He was a replacement for Earle Combs, who was out of the lineup with a shoulder injury. DiMaggio started well, banging out three hits, one of them a triple, in a game with the St. Louis Browns. In the next two games, against Detroit, he collected five more hits.

Joe also made a spectacular fielding play in the second game to preserve a 6–5 victory for the Yankees. With one out and men on first and third, Charley Gehringer whacked a long fly ball over DiMaggio's right shoulder. The graceful outfielder flew back and snatched the ball out of the air for out number two. The runner on third tagged up and streaked for the plate. But DiMaggio fired the ball to his catcher who caught the ball on the fly and in time to make the tag and end the inning. The young rookie could field as well as hit.

That fall, Joltin' Joe played against

Joe DiMaggio

the New York Giants in his first World Series. Again he made a spectacular showing, banging out nine hits—three of them doubles—to drive in three runs as the Yanks whipped the Giants in six games.

When the 1936 season was over, Yankee fans hoped that DiMaggio would be "another Ruth." But Joe was his own man and in the years that followed he showed that he was unforgettable in his own way.

A second rookie, Robert Feller, made as remarkable a debut as DiMaggio that same year. Feller went into the big leagues as a pitcher for the Cleveland Indians. In his first league game he struck out 15 St. Louis batsmen.

Bobby Feller was taught baseball by his father, a hard-working Iowa farmer. The elder Feller took time out from his daily chores to have the boy pitch to him as he stood with his back to the side of the barn. By the time Bobby was 10 years old, he could throw a baseball more than 275 feet.

As Bobby Feller grew older, his arm naturally got stronger. One daily workout ended when a pitch got past his father's glove and injured three ribs.

The Cleveland Indians signed Feller when he was 16 years old. Although he couldn't play in official games until he left high school, he often practiced with the Indians during the summer months.

On July 6, 1936, the St. Louis Cardinals—then leading the National League —visited Cleveland to play an exhibition game with the Indians. The dimple-cheeked right-hander, just 17, was scheduled to pitch three innings. Every eye in the ball park watched closely as the "kid" began to warm up. Soon, the crowd began to "ooooh" and "aaaaah" as Feller's fast ball exploded in the catcher's mitt.

The loud *thwack* of each Feller serve also had its effect on the Cards' second baseman, Frank Frisch. As Feller went to the mound, Frisch turned to teammate Stu Martin and said, "Stu, you're playing second today. I'm too old to get killed in the line of duty."

Feller proceeded to make the famed Gas House Gang look slightly ridiculous. The first batter he faced was thrown out on a bunt. The next, Leo Durocher, became his first major league strikeout victim. He then struck out the Cards' third baseman, Art Garibaldi.

In his second inning, Feller allowed a run on a single, two walks and a passed ball. But he also struck out three batters. In the third inning, he gave up a double and then proceeded to strike out the side. Thus, in his first three innings of major league ball, Bobby Feller gained eight of a possible nine outs by strikeouts. And he was still in high school.

Bob Feller

The next season, after graduation, Bobby returned to the Indians and soon became one of the greatest pitchers the game has ever seen.

A few years after DiMaggio and Feller appeared in the majors, a tall, gangling youngster arrived at the spring training camp of the Boston Red Sox. He immediately let everyone know he was ready to move into the Boston outfield as a starter. His name? Theodore "Ted" Williams.

At first base was old "double XX"— Jimmy Foxx. Foxx twice hit more than 50 homers a season and eventually placed second only to Ruth in total homers, with 534.

"Wait until you see Foxx hit, kid, and you'll think twice about taking this job," one of the Sox players cautioned Williams.

"Wait until Foxx sees *me* hit," Williams replied.

Williams didn't make the parent club that season and was sent to Minneapolis for seasoning. As he left, one of the older players said:

"So long, busher!"

"I'll be back," Williams retorted.

He was true to his word. Williams was on the Red Sox' roster in 1939, but his first two appearances at the plate weren't too promising. Yankee pitcher Red Ruffing struck him out twice on the same pitch.

Williams, always proud and sensitive about his hitting ability, vowed he would blast the ball out of the park if Ruffing threw him the same pitch again. Ruffing did exactly that. But

109

Ted Williams

Williams was ready. He took a vicious cut at the ball and drove it against the fence in right center field. It was his first major league hit, a double.

Williams hit 44 doubles, 11 triples and 31 homers in 1939. He also led the League in runs-batted-in with 145 and compiled a respectable .327 batting average. In his second year his homer total dropped to 23, but his average went up to .344. And in 1941 he hit for an amazing .406 average in 143 games, joining a select group of 12 other major leaguers who had hit .400 or better over a full season. No player since 1941 has approached Williams' .406 mark.

By the time he ended his playing career in 1960, Williams had compiled one of the most remarkable batting records in the history of the game. He earned the reputation of being base-

ball's foremost expert in the art of hitting.

The other great rookie of the era signed his first professional contract at about the same time Ted Williams began playing for Boston. He was Stan "The Man" Musial.

Stan Musial started as a pitcher-outfielder in the Mountain States League when he was 17 years old. One day while he was playing the outfield he tried to make a shoestring catch of a line drive. He took a tumble, crashing his shoulder into the ground. The accident almost finished him as a ball player, for his arm suddenly went dead. Later that season, the arm came back to life. By that time Stan had convinced his manager that he would be more valuable as an outfielder than as a pitcher. He was batting .369. Promoted to Rochester in the International League, he hit .327. Manager Billy Southworth quickly brought him to the St. Louis Cardinals for the last month of 1941.

Stan made his major league debut against Boston. He popped up in his first at-bat, but singled and doubled before the end of the game, which the Cards won 3–2. He got one hit in his second game and went three-for-three in the third.

The Cards then faced Chicago and against the Cubs Musial demonstrated clearly that he was in the big leagues to stay. He got two doubles and two singles, stole a base, made two fine catches in left field and threw a runner out at the plate.

He got his final single in the ninth

inning with the score tied 5–5. Musial then went to second on an infield out and the next batter walked. The next Card batsman managed to nudge the ball a few feet in front of the plate. The catcher scooped it up and threw to first, but the umpire ruled that the runner was safe.

The Cubs began arguing about the call, but no one called "time out." Stan took advantage of the situation and headed for third base. By the time the Cubs' first baseman, Babe Dahlgren, finally woke up, Musial was approaching home plate. Dahlgren's throw was too late, and Stan scored the winning run.

In his first full year with the Cards, Stan hit a respectable .315. In his second year he led the National League with .357. Like Williams, he became one of the game's best hitters, winning the National League batting title six more times.

The arrival of DiMaggio, Feller, Williams, and Musial in the majors ushered in a bright new day for baseball and its fans.

Stan Musial

40. Yankee Hearts

Although Joe McCarthy was fortunate enough to have a great collection of stars in Yankee flannels in the late thirties, he ran his ball club as a unit.

Some say he developed a machine that operated so efficiently he only had to push a button to win a ball game.

The Yankees, if one looks at the record, certainly did seem to have a machine-like quality. For they won four pennants between 1936 and 1939. And their World Series record of the same period reads as follows:

New York Yankees 4 games, New York Giants 2 games

New York Yankees 4 games, New York Giants 1 game

New York Yankees 4 games, Cincinnati Reds 0

New York Yankees 4 games, Chicago Cubs 0

Four pennants and four World Championships in a row! Only three losses in 19 World Series games played.

But Joe McCarthy was not a "push-button manager," for it takes great skill to handle a large group of talented ball players. It isn't easy to keep them happy and to keep them winning. As for the ball players, they need more than mechanical ability to win consistently. It takes spirit, unselfishness, and courage.

One man above all others proved just how human the Yankees of the late thirties were. He was Lou Gehrig.

In 1936—at the start of the Yanks' winning streak—Gehrig led the American League in home runs with 49. And he batted a sparkling .354. The next year Joe DiMaggio took the title by hitting 46 homers.

By the following season Gehrig's batting average and homer production had dropped considerably. At first Lou and the Yankees weren't too concerned.

"Lou's just had a bad year," was the general opinion.

When the next season began, though, it became clear that something was wrong with Lou. His play was ragged and grew more so as the schedule wore on. For the first time pitchers found it easy to strike him out.

Still Joe McCarthy didn't have the heart to bench the proud slugger.

Finally, on May 2, Lou spoke to his manager.

"Joe, I'm out of the lineup. I'm just not doing the team any good."

It was a painful moment for both men. But neither could deny the truth of Gehrig's words.

That was the day, of course, that Lou Gehrig established his all-time record of having played in 2,130 consecutive games. While he set many other records, it is this rugged performance that will be remembered longest.

But what was wrong with the Iron Horse? He was still a young man. He should have had many playing years left.

Lou set out to find the answer. Doctors discovered he had a rare and dread disease: amytrophic lateral sclerosis. A severe form of polio, it is now called "Gehrig's disease."

Right after he took himself out of the lineup, Lou's health worsened rapidly. The Yankees pretended not to notice.

On July 4, 1939, there was a "Lou Gehrig Day" at Yankee Stadium. All the old members of the superb 1927 team were brought together for the occasion. They gathered about Gehrig in the outfield, watching proudly as the 1927 pennant was drawn to the top of the flagpole. Then, along with the crowd, they listened with approval as each of the many dignitaries on the field spoke in glowing terms of their stricken former teammate.

Gehrig stood with head bowed, hands thrust deep into the rear pockets of his uniform pants. Occasionally he scratched the turf with one spiked shoe, then the other.

Suddenly the microphone was thrust at Lou. Hushed thousands waited for him to speak. But the broad-shouldered Yankee only gulped and kept his eyes fastened to the ground.

Joe McCarthy stepped forward quickly, patted Lou on the back, and spoke to him softly. It seemed to many that Joe was saying, as he had during many a tough spot in a ball game, "Come on, boy, you can do it!"

Some say Lou had carefully prepared a speech the night before. If so, he apparently decided against using it. For when he responded to McCarthy's urging and looked at the row upon row of faces that walled the park, he said simply:

"What young man wouldn't give anything to mingle with such men for a single day as I have for all these years?

Manager Joe McCarthy pats "The Iron Man" on the back.

Babe Ruth throws his arms around the big first baseman.

You've been reading about my bad breaks for weeks now. But today I think I'm the luckiest man alive. I now feel more than ever that I have much to live for."

When Gehrig finished speaking, Babe Ruth threw his arms around the big first baseman and hugged him. Gehrig's sincere, humbled words and Ruth's impulsive gesture warmed every heart and brought tears to many pairs of eyes.

There are those who believe Gehrig knew he was dying as he spoke at the Stadium that memorable day. If this is true, his brief speech points up the selflessness and bravery of the man.

Lou turned in his uniform after the World Series. He died less than two years later, but his magnificent playing record lives on.

41. The Daffiness Boys

In Brooklyn people were talking about the Dodgers—but for all the wrong reasons. The ball club that had won pennants in 1916 and 1920 wasn't doing very well.

According to baseball folklore, two Brooklyn fans sat in the bleachers on a sunny summer afternoon. One was anxiously watching the diamond, where the Dodgers had launched a sudden rally against the Giants. The other was working over his scorecard.

"Hey! Look!" shouted the first one, shoving an elbow into his friend's ribs. "The Dodgers have three men on base!"

His friend didn't even look up.

"Yeah?" he asked casually. "Which base?"

Such was the attitude of the large and loyal Brooklyn following in the years between 1920 and 1940. For these were the "Daffiness Days," when anything could happen in Brooklyn—and usually did.

In the twenties Floyd "Babe" Herman was one of the most erratic of the Brooklyn base runners. Without doubt he can be blamed for inspiring the three-men-on-a-base story recounted above. In 1926 Herman got involved in one of the most confounding plays imaginable. It happened during a double-header played against the Boston Braves at Brooklyn.

Brooklyn's Hank DeBerry was on third, Dazzy Vance was on second, and Chick Fewster was on first when Herman came to bat. Herman, always a wonderful hitter, bashed the ball to right field, where it caromed off the wall. DeBerry scored. Vance moved to third, deciding to take only one base. But Fewster took two bases, arriving at third with Vance. Herman, a little more ambitious than anyone else, took three bases. Suddenly there were three men on third base! They didn't stay there long, however. When Herman slid into third, Fewster jumped over his legs and was called out for passing a base runner. Then, since Vance was the only one entitled to hold third,

The Dodgers' Babe Herman at bat during a practice session.

"Uncle Robbie" displays a trophy—a golf trophy!—for the benefit of his daffy Dodgers.

Herman was declared out when the Braves' third baseman tagged him with the ball. In spite of the incident the Brooklyn team whipped the Braves in both games by scores of 4–2 and 11–3.

On another occasion, Herman drove a ball to the outfield with a runner on first. Herman was sure he had a double. He put his head down, raced to first, and turned for second.

The other runner, however, got as far as second, then realized the ball might be caught. Quick as a flash he spun around and headed back to first. He and Herman passed each other going in *opposite directions!*

Wilbert Robinson was at the Brooklyn helm during a great part of the "Daffiness Days." The old Oriole catcher was so good-humored and easy-going that everyone spoke of him as "Uncle Robbie." And the Brooklyn players, in those days, were called the "Robins" in his honor.

Although the team lolled in sixth place most of the time, it did have a few really good ball players on the roster. Actually Babe Herman himself was a much maligned ball player. He was an excellent hitter, once batting .393 for the Dodgers. And pitcher Dazzy Vance was another fine player. He had joined the team after spending 11 years in the minors. Vance led the League in strikeouts seven seasons in a row. In 10 years with Brooklyn, he whiffed 2,045 batters. One year he struck out 262 while winning 28 games.

As a team, though, Brooklyn was pretty poor. They made a brief comeback in 1930 when for 75 days they held first place in the National League. But by the end of the season they were down to fourth place. Robinson was demoted from president to just plain manager. The next year Brooklyn stayed in fourth place, and Robbie resigned at the end of the season.

The fumbling management tried several cures. They even brought back a one-time Brooklyn player, Casey Stengel, to act as coach and then as team manager. But the Dodgers slipped back to sixth place. Even the loyal fans stopped turning out to watch the "Daffiness Boys."

At the beginning of the 1934 season a sports writer asked Bill Terry, playing manager of the Giants, what he thought about Brooklyn's chances.

"Brooklyn?" Terry snapped. "Are they still in the League?"

Terry was to regret that remark. On the last Saturday of the season the Giants played the Dodgers at the Polo Grounds. Fifty thousand Brooklynites were screaming: "Is Brooklyn still in the league? You'll find out today, you bum."

And Terry did find out—the Dodgers beat the Giants 5–1. The following day they beat them again—8–5. Because of the fierce fight put up by the Dodgers the unfortunate Giants lost the pennant to the Cardinals.

By the beginning of the 1939 season the Dodger management had made really sweeping changes. Larry MacPhail, the man who had brought night baseball to Cincinnati, was the new president of the club. A tough shortstop by the name of Leo Durocher had taken over as manager.

117

Despite his ability as a fast, loud talker, Leo Durocher fails to change the umpire's decision.

Leo Durocher had started in the majors as an infielder with the New York Yankees. While not a .300 hitter, he was dangerous at the plate with men on base. In the field he was slick and quick.

Durocher talked so fast, so loudly, and so often that sports writers called him "Leo the Lip." His brashness and his talent for picking fights caused the Yankees to send him packing to the National League, where he played with the Reds and Cardinals before joining the Dodgers.

As a manager, Durocher was a throwback to John McGraw. He bullied the umpires and constantly flayed his opponents with his brassy voice and quick tongue. Although his manners were not the best, he knew how to excite his ball club and keep it moving.

By the end of the 1940 season the Dodgers had fought their way to second place in the National League, and they had won 16 out of 21 games with the Giants. From all over Brooklyn came the cry: "Wait till next year!"

And sure enough, 1941 proved to be the year the Dodgers finally won their third pennant. Although they lost the World Series to the Yankees in five games, they made one thing quite clear. The daffiness days were over.

42. The Post-War Comeback

From 1942 through 1945, professional baseball suffered from both lack of players and lack of fans. For these were the years when America was fighting in World War II. As scores of players changed from flannels to khaki and navy blue, the quality of major league baseball dropped very low indeed. And thousands of devoted fans were away fighting on far-flung fronts throughout the world.

With the end of the war, however, the big league stars streamed back to their ball clubs, and the fans turned out as never before.

Despite a long tour of military duty, Ted Williams batted .342 in the 1946 season. He also hit 38 homers, helping the Red Sox to run away with the pennant. In the 1946 All-Star game, Williams put on a show that almost equaled that of Carl Hubbell in 1934. In four turns at bat Williams hit two homers and two singles.

In the National League, the Cardinals and Dodgers fought a day-by-day battle for the pennant. Although the Cards were favored, Leo Durocher had the Dodgers so fired up they played a spectacular brand of ball.

On the last day of the season, the Dodgers played Boston at Ebbets Field, while the Cardinals played the Cubs in Chicago. The teams were tied for first place. The Dodgers lost and so did the Cards.

In the first play-off in National League history, the Cardinals downed Brooklyn in two games in a best-of-three series.

One of the returned Cardinal players was Stan Musial. He won his second batting title with .365. He seemed to have his best days when playing against Brooklyn. The Cardinals also benefitted from good pitching by Murry Dickson and Harry "The Cat" Brecheen. Dickson led the League with a 15-6 record.

In World Series play the Cards were at their best, beating the hard-hitting Red Sox in seven thrilling games. Brecheen won three games and allowed but one earned run in twenty innings.

Two American League pitchers—the Tigers' "Prince" Hal Newhouser and the Indians' Bobby Feller—each won twenty-six games that year. Feller also struck out 348 batters. This broke the record of 343 strike-outs in one season set by the eccentric Rube Waddell 42 years earlier.

Baseball had returned with a new punch!

43. A New Star for the Dodgers

While the major leagues were getting back to normal in 1946, something unusual happened in the International League. On opening day in Jersey City's Roosevelt Stadium a Negro played second base for the Montreal Royals. His name was Jackie Robinson. The 27-year-old, California-born Robinson had been signed to a Royals contract shortly after the 1945 World Series. Until that day Negroes had been kept out of professional baseball because of racial prejudice. The man who dared to sign up Robinson was Branch Rickey, who was now the general manager of the Brooklyn Dodgers. The Dodger organization used the Montreal Royals as a training ground.

Jackie Robinson was a remarkable athlete. He excelled in track, football, and basketball in high school and college. A highly intelligent player, he was also a determined competitor.

Before he finished college, Robinson went into the Army, serving as a 2nd lieutenant. Following that, he began playing baseball with the Kansas City Monarchs, an all-Negro team. It was there that Branch Rickey found him.

In his first game at Roosevelt Stadium, Robinson made it clear he had the potential of a big league star. He hit a homer and two singles, stole two bases, and scored four runs as the Royals won 14 to 1.

By the end of the season, Jackie had won the International League batting title. He also outshone every second baseman in the League in fielding and all-around play. More important, he was

Branch Rickey signs up Jackie Robinson for his second season.

Robinson, a whizz on the base paths, makes it home—minus his hat!

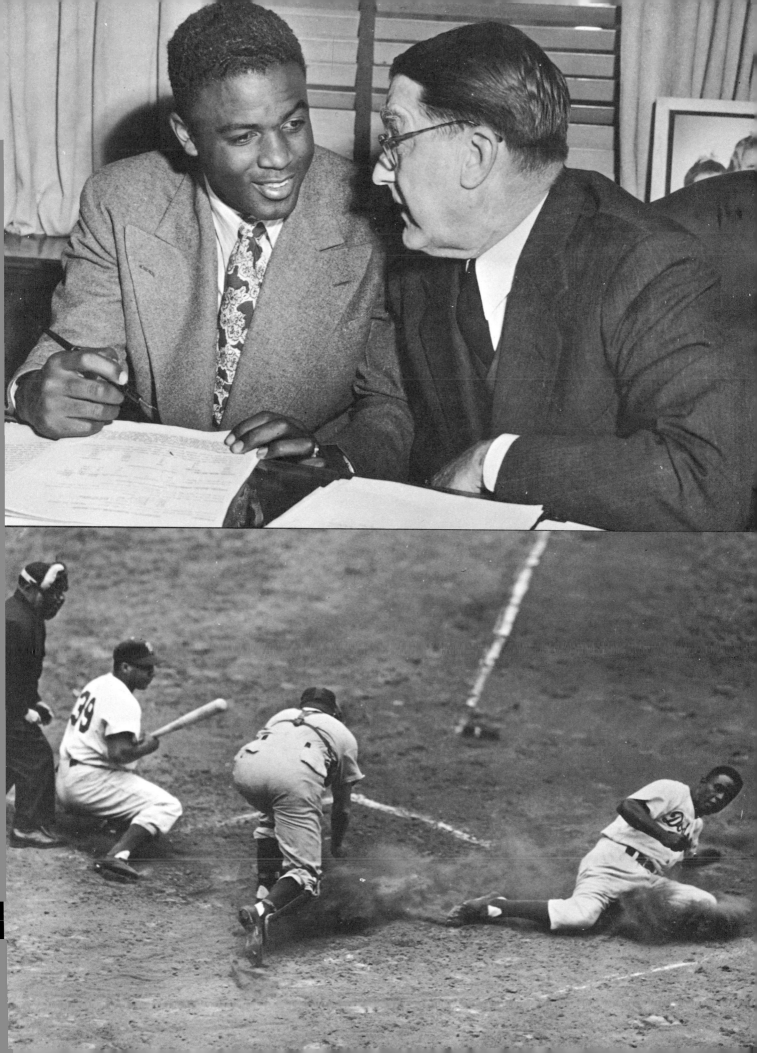

cheered wildly by the fans. And his teammates liked him.

Jackie's success was so spectacular that Branch Rickey had him report to the Dodgers the next season. He played a new position—first base—so that veteran Eddie Stanky could remain at second.

All but a few of the Dodgers accepted Jackie. But players on other teams, notably the Phillies and Cardinals, taunted him unmercifully. At one point the Cardinals threatened to strike if Robinson was in the lineup against them.

But Cardinal owner Sam Breadon quickly put a stop to the threat. Breadon's hand was strengthened by National League President Ford Frick, who said he would suspend anyone who struck over the issue of Robinson's playing, "even if it means wrecking the League.

"This is the United States of America and one player has as much right to play as another," Frick said sternly.

Robinson had promised Rickey that he would ignore the bench jockeying and concentrate on his game. Through great effort he kept his word. It was the right formula, too. For in that first year with the Dodgers, Robinson won the "Rookie of the Year" title and batted .296.

In 1949 Robinson won the batting title, and was named the Most Valuable Player in the National League. He led the League twice in stolen bases and three times in fielding, and became one of the great stars of the game before he retired.

44. The Yanks Again

The Dodgers played the 1947 season under a new manager, Burt Shotton. Shotton was an old-time baseball man, and he led the Brooklyn team to another pennant.

In the American League it was the New York Yankees again. They built a heavy attack around Joe DiMaggio, who won the 1947 Most Valuable Player award in the American League. The Yankees had fine pitching to go with the hitting. Allie Reynolds, for example, was the best in the majors with an 18-5 record.

The Yankees also developed a remarkable relief pitcher in Joe Page, a happy-go-lucky left-hander who reminded the fans of Dizzy Dean. Like Dean, Page used but one method to snuff out a batting rally. He would rear back and fire the ball toward the plate as hard as he could.

The 1947 World Series was remarkable in many ways. At the gate the Yan-

kees and the Dodgers drew almost 390,-
000 fans as the Series went to seven
games. But many more thousands "saw"
the game, for that year the Bell Tele-
phone System opened the nation's
first television network. It linked
New York, Philadelphia, Baltimore, and
Washington.

The Series itself was full of thrills.
Few games, however, matched the fourth
for sheer drama. The Yankees, playing
in Ebbets Field, were leading in games
by 2 to 1. By the bottom of the ninth in
the fourth game they were ahead 2 to 1
in score. More important, Yankee pitcher
Floyd "Bill" Bevens had a no-hitter
going.

Bevens walked outfielder Carl Furillo
to put the tying run on base. Burt Shotton replaced Furillo with Al Gionfriddo,
another outfielder. Gionfriddo was a
small man with the speed of a jack rab-
bit. With Pete Reiser at the plate, he
promptly stole second. The Yankee manager, Bucky Harris, then had Bevens
walk Reiser, even though Reiser represented the winning run.

Eddie Stanky was the Dodgers' next
hitter, but Shotton substituted Cookie
Lavagetto, a third baseman who was at
his best with runners on base. Lavagetto came through with a double to
right field which crashed high against
the scoreboard. Bevens lost his no-hitter and the ball game.

The Yanks crushed the Dodgers 5-2
in the seventh game, and won the Series. Joe Page was the hero of that victory. He came in from the bull pen and
pitched 1-hit ball for the last five
innings.

A Yankee World Series hero, Joe Page, is congratulated by big boss Larry MacPhail (right) and teammate Joe DiMaggio (left).

45. The Pick-off

The records show that Bobby Feller was the hardest working pitcher of his day. He led the majors in the number of innings pitched for five years.

But Feller had the misfortune to play with the Cleveland Indians, a team that hadn't won a pennant since 1920. In 1948, however, it seemed that Feller and the rest of the Indians might finally have a chance to get into a World Series.

To do it, the Indians had to overcome two powerful opponents—the New York Yankees and the Boston Red Sox. These two teams were being kept in the thick of the fight by two of the best hitters in baseball—Joe DiMaggio and Ted Williams. DiMaggio hit 39 homers to lead the American League, while Williams won the batting title with .369.

Feller, Gene Bearden, Mike Garcia, and Bob Lemon were the backbone of the Indians' mound corps. The team's batting punch came from dark-haired Lou Boudreau, the shortstop and manager.

The American League flag race couldn't have been closer. The Indians and Red Sox ended in a tie. In a one-game play-off, Boudreau rocked Boston by batting two homers. The Indians won 8 to 3.

While the Indians fought their way to the flag in the American League, an interesting race developed in the National.

The St. Louis Cardinals had two players who took top individual honors in two departments. Stan Musial was the National League's leading hitter with 39 homers and a .376 batting average. His teammate, Harry "The Cat" Brecheen, was the best pitcher in the league with a 20–7 record.

Despite the great play of Musial and Brecheen, the Cards couldn't quite make it. For the Boston Braves had two pitchers who seemed unbeatable—Warren Spahn and John Sain. So regularly did this pair win that the Boston fans claimed the Braves could take the pennant all over again if the pitchers got sufficient rest. The formula, they said, was "Spahn, Sain and two days of Rain."

Manager Lou Boudreau warmed the hearts of ball fans everywhere by naming the hard-working Feller to pitch the World Series opener against Sain. The choice wasn't based entirely on sentiment. For although Feller had lost the booming fast ball that once enabled him to establish the all-time record of striking out 18 hitters in one game, he was still a mighty effective pitcher.

In place of the fast ball, Feller had developed one of the biggest and best curves the majors had ever seen. Above all, Boudreau knew Feller had a fighting heart.

As Sain and Feller dueled away, it seemed no one would score. The Braves' Phil Masi, however, got to second. As Feller "stretched" to pitch to Tommy Holmes, Masi took a long lead. Cleveland fans nudged each other.

"Watch this," they chortled. "Watch this!"

They were looking for the famous pick-off play that the Cleveland pitchers and Boudreau had used all season. Feller

Lou Boudreau looks at the umpire with surprise as Phil Masi is declared safe at second.

The Boston Braves had two pitchers who were almost unbeatable—southpaw Warren Spahn (left) and righty John Sain.

took a quick look at Masi, then turned away. At that instant the pick-off signal had been passed. Boudreau dashed to second behind Masi. Feller whirled and threw the ball to him as Masi scrambled desperately to get back to the base.

"He's out! He's out!" the Cleveland fans yelled delightedly.

But no! The umpire had flung his hands sideward, palms down.

"Safe!" the hands signaled.

The call was hotly disputed then—and it still is today. The Braves' Tommy Holmes proceeded to get Masi home on a single, and Bobby Feller lost his first World Series game 1–0.

Although Feller lost the fifth game 11 to 5, the Indians won the sixth and final game 4–3 by dint of the fine pitching of Bearden and Lemon. They also won the Series.

It was Feller's only appearance in a World Series.

46. The Newcomers

Each generation produces its own great names, whether in politics, science, the arts, or sports. With the close of the 1940s and the beginning of the 1950s, a new wave of stars swept across the diamond, keeping interest in baseball fresh and very much alive.

One of these was Warren Spahn, the six-foot left-hander who helped pitch the Boston Braves to a pennant in 1948. Spahn had joined the Braves in 1942, but went into military service and did

not pitch his first big league game until 1946, when he won eight and lost five.

Spahn soon developed uncanny control and a wide assortment of pitches. Between 1947 and 1965 he posted 20 or more victories in each of 13 seasons and wound up with a total of 363 wins, placing fifth in the all-time list of winningest pitchers. Moving with the Braves from Boston to Milwaukee, he became a hero in the Braves' pennant drives in 1957 and 1958.

Breaking in with the Yankees in 1946 was another rugged player, Lawrence "Yogi" Berra, a jug-eared catcher who was built like a fire plug, but who had surprising ability at bat and in the field. Berra was to spend 19 years in the majors, knocking in more than 100 runs in a season five times. Three times he was named the American League's Most Valuable Player. He also appeared in a record 75 World Series games in 14 years. His World Series records include 259 at-bats, 71 hits and 10 doubles.

Berra's most famous battery mate and another outstanding player of the period was Edward "Whitey" Ford. Like Spahn, he was a left-handed control pitcher who was toughest when the chips were down. Joining the Yankees in 1950, Ford pitched for 16 years, piling up 236 victories. Like Berra, he became best known for his play in 11 World Series. He established a number of World Series records, starting 22 games, pitching 146 innings and winning ten times.

Coming into the majors in 1951 were two of the most remarkable center fielders of all time—Mickey Mantle of the New York Yankees and Willie Mays of the New York Giants (later the San Francisco Giants).

Mantle, a blond, bull-shouldered switch hitter, could blast the ball for tremendous distances from either side of the plate. He also had a fine throwing arm and great speed—he could travel from home to first base in 3.1 seconds. In 18 injury-riddled seasons with the Yankees, Mantle hit a total of 536 homers and, like Berra, was thrice

named the American League's Most Valuable Player. He hit .300, .306, .353, .365 and .304 in the five seasons between 1954 and 1958. In this period, he also averaged 38 homers a year and drove in more than 100 runs each season.

Unlike Mantle, whose career was cut short by injuries, Mays was still going strong in 1971 at the age of 40. By that

The old star and the new—Joe DiMaggio (left) poses with Mickey Mantle.

time, he had collected 646 homers, second only to Babe Ruth's 714. Some of Mays' best seasons, too, were in the 1950s. Coming out of two years of military service in 1954, for example, he hit 41 homers, collected 110 RBI's and won the National League batting title with a sparkling .345 average. He was named the National League's Most Valuable Player. In 1955 he drove in 127 runs and hit 51 homers. Like Mantle, Willie also had speed and daring on the basepaths. He led the league in stolen bases four straight years between 1956 and 1959. Beginning in 1959, he drove in more than 100 runs eight years in a row, although he never quite managed to win the RBI title.

128   Three years after the arrival of Mays

Rookie Willie Mays slides home safely against the Dodgers (top), and a few years later young Hank Aaron comes home after hitting a 400-foot homer (right).

and Mantle, another remarkable out-fielder became a major leaguer. He was Henry Aaron. A medium-sized right-hand hitter with powerful wrists, Aaron was often compared to Rogers Hornsby. He joined the National League Braves in 1954, a year after the team had moved from Boston to Milwaukee. He got off to a modest start, hitting .280, notching 13 homers and 69 RBI's. From then on, however, he terrorized National League pitchers. Going into the 1970s, he had averaged more than 30 home runs and more than 100 RBI's a year. His lifetime batting average was above .300.

By 1971, Aaron was third in career home runs with 639. He seemed likely to pass Willie Mays and some felt he had a chance to break Ruth's awesome record of 714 before he retired.

Yes, the newcomers—and especially these five—added much to the baseball world as the game moved through the 1950s.

47. A Perfect Marriage

When the New York Yankees finished third in 1948, the owners of the team fired manager Bucky Harris. The Yankees were used to finishing first, so no one was surprised that Harris was let go. But the appointment of Casey Stengel as the new manager really set tongues wagging.

"That clown?" the fans asked. "Manage the Yankees?"

Casey had been a fair major league ballplayer and he had had years of experience managing—but all the teams he had managed in the majors had been losers. Casey was most famous as an entertainer and a clown, not as a winner. His coming to the Yankees was like a country bumpkin marrying a glamorous movie queen—the match seemed un-likely to last, let alone succeed.

But those who scoffed at Casey over-looked something. He had learned his baseball from such men as John McGraw and Wilbert Robinson. He knew more about the game than most people ever learn. And he knew how to get the most from the players he worked with.

In 1949, Casey's first year, the Yankees clung to the heels of the hot Boston Red Sox despite a long series of injuries to key players. On the last day of the season, the Sox were to play a doubleheader with the Yanks. If the Yanks could win both games they would take the championship.

Ted Williams was having another good year. He led the League in homers with 43 and lost the batting title by but a fraction of a percentage point. The Sox' best pitchers—Ellis Kinder and Mel Parnell—were rested and ready for the Yanks. But the Yankees upset all the odds. They won the two games and the pennant.

The first two games of the Yankees-Dodgers World Series were as tight as the pennant races. The Yankees won the opener 1 to 0 on a homer by Tom "Old Reliable" Henrich. The Dodgers won the second game by the same score on a double by Jackie Robinson and a single by Gil Hodges.

But the Yankees won the next three to give Casey Stengel his first World Championship. It was just a hint of things to come.

In 1950, with Joe DiMaggio and shortstop Phil Rizzuto having great years at bat and pitcher Vic Raschi's 21–8 record tops in the League, the Yanks again took the flag, this time fighting off Detroit and Boston. As for the World Series, the Yanks beat the Phils four straight.

The Yankees toss manager Casey Stengel in the air after winning the American League Pennant.

Boston and Cleveland were the main threats to the Yankees in 1951. Ted Williams again powered the Boston attack, while Bobby Feller proved to be the best in the League and one of three pitchers to win 20 or more games for Cleveland.

The Yankees had two 21-game winners in Vic Raschi and Eddie Lopat. Allie Reynolds also pitched two no-hitters. But hitting was very weak. Only one player—Gil McDougald, a rookie infielder—hit over .300. Yogi Berra, however, had 88 runs batted in to lead the team.

The Yanks suffered a severe blow when Joe DiMaggio, their star center fielder, was injured toward the close of the year. To replace him, Stengel daringly dipped into the Yankee farm system and called on a blond, converted shortstop. He was Mickey Mantle.

Overcoming all their shortcomings, the Yankees finished five games ahead of Cleveland and 11 in front of Boston. The World Series with the Giants went to six games. But the results were the same as in the previous two years.

As the following season got underway, fans and sportswriters suddenly realized that Casey and the Yanks had a chance to tie a record by winning four pennants in a row. This had only been accomplished twice before, by Joe McCarthy's 1936–39 Yankees and John McGraw's 1921–24 New York Giants. McCarthy's teams had also won four straight World Series.

To take the pennant in 1952, the Yanks had to fight off Cleveland's powerful pitching staff of three 20-game

Mickey Mantle receives the congratulations of his teammates after hitting a grand slam homer in the 1953 World Series.

winners—Early Wynn, Bob Lemon and Mike Garcia. They also had to overcome the Chicago White Sox.

Surprisingly, the Philadelphia Athletics caused some trouble, too. The A's had a tiny left-hander, Bobby Shantz, who won 24 games, while first baseman Ferris Fain became the League's leading hitter with a .327 average.

But the Yankees did win the pennant, even though Mickey Mantle and outfielder Gene Woodling were the only two players to hit over .300. They then triumphed over the Dodgers in the Series to tie the McCarthy-Yankee record of the 1930s.

Now that they had tied the record, could Stengel's Yankees do what had never been done before—capture the pennant and the Series for the fifth time in a row?

The answer was a resounding "yes!"

The 1953 Yankees, stronger than the year before, won the pennant easily, finishing in front by 8½ games. Lefty Edward "Whitey" Ford and Eddie Lopat won 34 games between them.

In the Series a man named Martin dominated the play. He was Billy Martin, the Yankees' aggressive second baseman. He hit two homers, two triples, a double and seven singles as the Yankees won in six games. Mickey Mantle swung a potent bat, too, driving in seven runs with five hits.

The Yankees threatened to make it six in a row in 1954, but the Indians, still getting great pitching from Wynn, Lemon and Garcia, beat them out. To do it, however, Cleveland had to win 111 games, a new record for the American League.

Over the next six years, Casey's Yankees won five more American League titles. Their record of ten pennants and seven World Series victories in twelve years (1949–1960) made them the dominant team of the 1950s and the most successful baseball dynasty in history. The unlikely marriage between Stengel and the Yanks turned out to be just about perfect.

48. "Wait Till Next Year"

During the late 1940s and throughout the 1950s, the Dodgers—playing first in Brooklyn and later in Los Angeles—became for the National League what the New York Yankees had long been for the American—the team to beat.

In the 13 seasons between 1947 and 1959, the once apathetic and comical Dodgers won seven League championships, finished second three times and third twice.

Unlike the mighty Yankees, however, the Dodgers usually faced stiff opposition. In 1949, for example, they had the League's leading hitter in Jackie Robinson and the top pitcher in the circuit in Elwin "Preacher" Roe. Still, they were unable to nail down the pennant until the last day of the season, when they defeated Philadelphia and beat out the hard-fighting Cardinals by one game.

In 1950 the tables were turned. The Brooks lost the pennant on the final day.

The winners were the Phillies, a team so young they were dubbed the "Whiz Kids." Skillfully managed by Eddie Sawyer, a former Yankee farm hand and a science professor at Ithaca College in the off-season, the Phillies had the services of three outstanding pitchers—left-hander Curt Simmons, right-hander Robin Roberts and right-hander Jim Konstanty.

Roberts, regarded by many as the best right-hander to ever wear a Phillies uniform, won 20 games, second in the League to the Braves' Warren Spahn, who notched 21 victories. Simmons won 17, while relief specialist Konstanty led the League with 22 "saves" in a remarkable 74 appearances.

Things seemed to be different for the Dodgers the following year. For on August 11, they were out in front by 13½ games. But their bitterest rival, the New York Giants, managed by Leo

Durocher, began to close the gap. When they met the Dodgers on September 1 for a two-game series, they were riding a 16-game winning streak. The Giants won both games. Jim Hearn and Sal Maglie hurled masterfully for New York, while right fielder Don Mueller hit five homers to drive in almost all the Giant runs.

The Giants continued to creep up on the Dodgers and with one game left, the two teams were tied. The Giants would be playing the Braves and Brooklyn was at Philadelphia.

The Dodger game began as a disaster. The Phils knocked Preacher Roe out of the box and took a 6–1 lead. But the Dodgers fought back to tie the score in the eighth inning. At this point word arrived that the Giants had beaten the Braves—if the Dodgers lost the game they would also lose the pennant.

In the twelfth inning, Philadelphia loaded the bases with two out. First baseman Eddie Waitkus, a left-handed batter, drove a liner between first baseman Gil Hodges and second baseman Jackie Robinson.

Robinson, starting with Waitkus' swing, hurled his body to his left and speared the ball no more than an inch from the ground. It was probably the greatest catch of his career.

Thus the game remained tied in the thirteenth. At the top of the fourteenth, Robinson smacked out a homer to give the Dodgers the winning margin and a tie for the pennant.

The thrills didn't end there, though. A three-game play-off was arranged, with the opener to be held at Ebbets Field. The Dodgers led with their ace right-hander, Ralph Branca. Branca went crashing to defeat when the Giants' Bobby Thomson cracked a two-run homer into the seats.

The Brooklyn team evened matters by taking the second game 10 to 0 behind pitcher Clem Labine.

Don Newcombe was the Brooklyn choice to oppose Larry Jansen in the dramatic "third" game. The Brooks quickly scored off Jansen and by the ninth inning were leading 4 to 1. Three outs and the game would be over. Brooklyn would be the champion of the National League.

But fate was taking a different turn. Shortstop Alvin Dark opened the inning for the Giants with a single. He then went to third on another single by Don Mueller. Monte Irvin grounded out, but Whitey Lockman doubled. The Lockman hit scored one run, making the total 4 to 2. It also put runners on second and third and brought the winning run to the plate in the form of Bobby Thomson.

At this tense moment the Brooklyn manager made the fans buzz by replacing Newcombe with Ralph Branca.

"Doesn't he remember what Thomson did the last time?" one Brooklyn fan yelled.

"Yeah, but it can't happen again," another responded.

With the crowd tense and roaring with every move, Branca took his warm-up tosses. Finally he was ready. He stepped on the rubber, looked at the runners, and poured his fast ball toward the plate.

"Stuh-r-r-ri-i-ke!" the ump yelled.

The ball came back to Branca. The graceful right-hander rubbed it carefully, dried his fingers on the rosin bag, tugged at his cap, and then went back to the pitching plate. He took his stretch, again checked the runners, then fired to the waiting Thomson.

C-R-A-C-K!

The instant the bat hit the ball, the crowd knew. Called "the shot heard 'round the world," it was one of the most thrilling homers in baseball. Thomson's hit had won the game and the pennant for the Giants. For the second year in a row the Dodgers had lost everything on the last day.

When Brooklyn lost to the Phils in 1950 and to the Giants in 1951, Dodger fans repeated a cry that was to become their trademark:

"Wait till next year!"

The Dodgers jumped away to a big lead in 1952. Then toward the end of the season the Giants began to close in again. It looked like a repeat of 1951. But this time, the Giants lacked the strength and their challenge failed.

"Leave us at the Yankees!" the Brooklyn fans cried, recalling that the American League champions had defeated the Brooks in the 1941, 1947 and 1949 Series.

The 1952 Series went the full seven games, but once again the Dodgers couldn't bring the Yankees down.

Again the old cry went up:

"Wait till next year!"

The next year arrived and the Dodgers' chances of winning a World Championship looked better than ever. They ran away with the National League pennant. At one point, the club won 41 out of 50 games. Carl Furillo, one of five regulars to hit over .300, won the National League batting title with .344.

But the Dodgers lost the Series to the Yankees again, this time in six games. Then in 1954 they lost the National League pennant to the Giants. Their fans were getting impatient with "next year."

The season was barely under way when all of Brooklyn became convinced that 1955 was the year. For Brooklyn's Gil Hodges, Roy Campanella, Carl Furillo, and Duke Snider pounded out hits as never before. Although the Dodger pitching was weak, the thunderous attack launched by these four players carried Brooklyn to a smashing National League victory—13½ games ahead of the pack. Duke Snider knocked out 42 home runs and drove in 135 runs, the top record in the League. Roy Campanella added 32 homers and batted in another 100 runs. This performance won him his third annual award as Most Valuable Player in the National League.

Toward the end of the year Walter Alston, a new Brooklyn manager, apparently had an eye turned in the direction of the World Series, for he brought three young pitchers to the Dodgers from the vast Brooklyn farm system. These included right-handers Don Bessent and Roger Craig and a remarkable left-hander, Johnny Podres.

The Yankees were up to their old tricks in the American League. They staged a tough fight and finally won out over Chicago, Cleveland, and the ever threatening Boston Red Sox.

134

A dejected Dodger, Roy Campanella, walks away from the plate after the Yankees' Hank Bauer (Number 9) chalks up the winning run in the sixth and deciding game of the 1953 World Series.

Next year comes at last as Johnny Podres (center) beats the Yankees in the seventh game of the 1955 Series.

The Dodgers seemed to have the better team, but little Whitey Ford and Bob Grim pitched the Yanks to a 6–5 victory over Brooklyn in the Series opener.

The wailing of Brooklyn fans reached a new high, as the Yanks won the second game 4 to 2. Johnny Podres made them feel a little better by taming the Yanks 8 to 3 in the third game. Then the Brooks proceeded to win games four and five. Suddenly the Series score stood at Brooklyn 3 games, Yankees 2 games. One more victory and Brooklyn would have its first World Championship.

But cool, clever Whitey Ford kept up the suspense by beating Brooklyn 5–1. One game remained.

Johnny Podres matched his left-handed pitches against the combined efforts of Bob Grim, Tommy Byrne, and

Bob Turley in the seventh game. Brooklyn started the scoring in the fourth inning as Campanella hit a double, then raced home on a single by Brooklyn's great first baseman, Gil Hodges. The Dodgers scored again in the sixth on a single, error, infield out, and sacrifice fly.

The most sensational play of the Series cropped up in the bottom of the sixth with the Yankees at bat. Billy Martin walked, Gil McDougald bunted his way on. This brought Yogi Berra to the plate with the lead run with only one out.

Since Berra was a left-handed batter who liked to "pull" the ball into right field, the Dodger outfield shifted to right to meet this threat. Naturally the shift opened a big hole in left field.

Mr. Berra must have had his eye on this hole, for he promptly cracked a curving fly ball into it. Martin and McDougald, sure that Yogi's poke would be good for at least a double, flew around the bases.

To the roaring amazement of the crowd, however, the Dodgers' left fielder, tiny Sandy Amoros, raced to his right. And after a breathtaking run he reached out and plucked the ball from the air. Without hesitating, he whirled and threw to relay man Pee Wee Reese. Reese fired to Gil Hodges at first, doubling up McDougald and ending the threat.

That play seemed to be all the encouragement young Podres needed. He bore down with his crackling fast ball and teasing change of pace. The Dodgers won their first World Championship.

"Next year" had arrived at last.

49. One of a Kind

As the years wear on, even the very greatest stars must finally give up the game and retire. Two of the great ones, Joe DiMaggio and Bobby Feller, hung up their spikes for good during the 1950s.

DiMaggio spent 13 years in the majors with the New York Yankees. As with many ballplayers of his generation, his career was shortened by several years in the armed forces during World War II. But when he retired after the 1951 season, his statistics would have honored a 20-year player—361 homers, 2,214 hits, 1,537 runs batted in, a .325 lifetime batting average and 54 hits in 51 World Series games.

While statistics are an important measure of a player's ability, they don't always tell the whole story. DiMaggio was a ballplayer's ballplayer. Making his first appearance in 1936, he quickly rose head and shoulders above any other outfielder of his time. DiMaggio was one of the most graceful players baseball has ever seen. He ran, he threw and he swung his bat with a rhythm and precision that has seldom been equaled.

Of all DiMaggio's feats, the one to attract the most attention occurred in 1941. During spring training, he got at least one base hit in each of the Yankees' last 19 games. He carried the streak into the regular season for eight more games before being held hitless. Counting exhibition and regular-season games, he had hit safely in 27 straight. But this was only a warm-up. DiMaggio singled off White Sox lefty Edgar Smith on May 15 to begin another consecutive hitting spree that has never been matched.

At the time, Rogers Hornsby held the "modern" record for the National League. He had hit safely in 33 games. Joltin' Joe passed this mark in mid-June.

DiMaggio comes home after hitting his last major league home run.

The American League record, 41 games, was set by George Sisler in 1922. On June 29, DiMaggio hit safely in his 42nd straight game to break Sisler's record.

The only mark left was the 44-game record set before baseball's "modern" era by Wee Willie Keeler of the 1897 Baltimore Orioles. This record fell on July 2, when DiMag clouted a home run against the Boston Red Sox' Heber Newsome. With that blow, Joe had hit safely in 45 consecutive games.

In 1955 Bob Feller pitches the 12th 1-hit game of his career.

DiMaggio's hitting streak drew huge crowds wherever the Yankees went. As each day passed, it got longer and longer —46, 47, 48, 49, 50 . . . Would it ever end? On July 16, Joe got three hits off two Cleveland pitchers, Al Milnar and Joe Krakauskas, marking game number 56. The next night, 67,468 came to the Cleveland ball park to see if he could make it 57.

Indian left-hander Al Smith got Joe out on two hard smashes to third baseman Ken Keltner. On his third time up Joe walked. Late in the game Joe came up for the last time against a knuckle baller, Jim Bagby, with two out and a man on first. He needed a hit to keep the streak going. Joe rapped a Bagby pitch at shortstop Lou Boudreau who threw to second to force the runner. The streak had ended at 56 games. But in the next thirty years no major leaguer even approached Joe's amazing record.

Like DiMaggio, Bob Feller also established a long list of significant statistics. In 18 years, the powerful right-hander won 266 games while losing 162. When he retired after the 1956 season, he had struck out 2,581 batters, and pitched three no-hitters, 12 one-hitters and 44 shutouts. In 1946 he broke Rube Waddell's season strikeout record by fanning 348. While 10 strikeouts a game is a high number for any pitcher, Feller struck out 15 or more several times.

During Feller's career, the Indians won the pennant only two times. But Bob always managed to be among the top pitchers in the American League. He led the League in strikeouts seven times, and in victories six times. He was also one of the hardest-working pitchers in the league, leading in innings pitched five times. Like DiMaggio, Feller lost several seasons at the height of his career, serving in the Navy through nearly four full seasons.

In 1969, when baseball celebrated its 100th birthday, Joe DiMaggio was named the "Greatest Living Player." Both DiMaggio and Feller were on the "Greatest Living Players Team." Those who saw them play agree that they were unforgettable. For, like all the greats, they were one of a kind.

50. Change

The years after 1945 were the most successful in baseball's history. Almost everywhere interest and attendance at the games were up. But as baseball moved into the 1950s, there were signs of trouble.

There were complex reasons for these new problems. Although Americans had more leisure time than ever, there were more ways to spend it. Automobile travel increased as never before. Boating, golf, camping, bowling—all of these activities grew rapidly and kept people away from the ballpark.

Television, which would soon be in nearly every American home, also had a big impact on the game. In some ways it helped, but in others it endangered baseball's health. Major league teams sold television rights to their games and television became an important new source of income.

But television was hard on the weaker major league clubs and it was a disaster for minor league baseball. In Boston, for instance, the fans preferred to watch the exciting Red Sox on television rather than go to see the second-division Braves. Since the television market wasn't large enough to support two teams, the Braves lost out.

Fans in minor league areas soon became used to seeing big league ball on TV and stopped going to see their local teams. Within a few years nearly half of the country's minor league teams were out of business.

Owners of troubled major league teams soon realized that there were many cities in America eager to have big league baseball. Although the population had been shifting to the west for years, all the big league baseball teams were still in the northeastern states. There were three teams in New York and two each in Boston, Philadelphia, Chicago and St. Louis. And yet there were no teams south of Washington, D.C., or west of St. Louis.

So the stage was set for changes in the major league system that had stood up for fifty years. The Boston Braves were the first to break the pattern, moving to Milwaukee in 1953. The team

Milwaukee Braves manager Fred Haney with his stars, Red Schoendienst and Hank Aaron.

enjoyed an enthusiastic and profitable reception.

Milwaukee set the style for the new major league cities. It gave the Braves the use of a new $5 million stadium with 35,000 seats and plenty of parking space. More important, it offered a large number of enthusiastic fans who were eager to welcome the big leaguers to their city.

The following year the St. Louis Browns, long holding second place to the Cardinals in St. Louis, moved to Baltimore and became the Orioles. In 1955 the Philadelphia Athletics also changed cities, but kept their nickname, becoming the Kansas City A's.

Then in the biggest move of all, the Brooklyn Dodgers and the New York Giants announced on the same day in 1958 that they would be moving to the West Coast—the Dodgers to Los Angeles and the Giants to San Francisco. For the first time, the big leagues would extend from coast to coast.

The move was a big shock to New Yorkers, however. Unlike earlier transplants, the two New York teams were healthy and were contenders for the pennant almost every year. Now all of a sudden, New York had only one team instead of three. The fans complained bitterly that they had been sold out by greedy owners.

One development that made the West Coast teams possible was that of reliable air travel. When the major leagues were started, the cities in the league had to be within easy reach by train. But air travel—especially the development of jet liners—made it possible for a team to be anywhere in the country in a few hours.

Not only were the new Milwaukee Braves the first to move. They also were the first to succeed. After they settled in their new surroundings, a great change came over the club. True, there were new faces in the lineup and new uniforms. But the change wasn't something that could be seen and touched. It was a change of spirit.

Some two million Milwaukee fans gave the Braves the kind of support rarely seen in big league history and the Braves responded gallantly. They finished second in 1953, third in 1954, second in 1955 and 1956. Then in 1957 they won the National League pennant.

Sparking the Braves' attack was Hank Aaron, voted the league's Most Valuable Player for 1957. He led the league with 44 home runs. Ageless Warren Spahn won 21 games while Lew Burdette and Bob Buhl ably assisted him in holding enemy batters in check.

The Braves faced the New York Yanks (who had won their third pennant in a row) in the World Series. Whitey Ford hurled the Yanks to victory in the opening game. But the Braves had an ace pitcher of their own. Lew Burdette won three games and pitched an amazing 24⅔ scoreless innings as the Braves won the Series in seven games.

Hank Aaron was just as effective during the Series as he was during the season. He collected eleven hits, three of them homers.

The Braves victory set off some of the wildest celebration in memory. Milwaukee, which had been so eager for big league ball, celebrated from dusk to dawn this first great victory of their team.

The new world champions made it clear that they were no fluke by winning the pennant again in 1958. The Dodgers, in their first year in Los Angeles, had lost their great catcher, Roy Campanella, when a tragic auto accident injured his spine and ended his career. Surprisingly, the biggest challenge to the Braves came from the Pittsburgh Pirates. But the Braves won strongly and faced the Yankees again in the World Series.

The Braves jumped ahead to a lead of three games to one against the Yanks and it looked as if they had the Series won. The Yankees kept their hopes alive by routing Lew Burdette 7–0 in the fifth game. The last two games were to be played in Milwaukee and the Braves needed only one to win.

At the end of nine innings in the sixth game the score was tied 2–2. The Yanks scored twice in the top of the tenth. In the bottom of the tenth the Braves scored one run and had the tying run

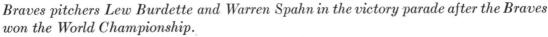

Braves pitchers Lew Burdette and Warren Spahn in the victory parade after the Braves won the World Championship.

141

on third when the inning ended. The Yanks had tied the Series at three games apiece.

Lew Burdette pitched the deciding seventh game. Going into the ninth inning it was another 2–2 tie. But Yogi Berra doubled, Elston Howard singled and Moose Skowron homered to make the score 5–2. The Braves couldn't match that burst in the bottom of the ninth. So the Yankees, winning the last three games in a row, took the world championship back to New York.

In 1959 the Braves finished the season in first place for the third year in a row. But so did another club—the Dodgers, who had just completed their second year in Los Angeles. The play-off series to determine the pennant winner was taken by the Dodgers in two straight games. They went on to defeat the White Sox in the World Series, bringing the world championship to still another new city.

Thus, the 1950s ended on a new note. With new teams in Milwaukee, Los Angeles, San Francisco, Baltimore and Kansas City, the major leagues had changed—and, according to most observers, changed for the better. One thing was predictable—there would be further changes in the future.

51. The Classics

Not every great accomplishment in baseball is the work of a superstar like DiMaggio or Feller. During the 1950s two of the most remarkable pitching feats in history were performed by men who will be remembered for what they did in a single game.

The first of these pitching classics came about in the 1956 World Series between the New York Yankees and the Brooklyn Dodgers.

The first game of the Series was won by Brooklyn, 6–3, behind the pitching of Sal "The Barber" Maglie, a veteran right-hander. In the second game the Brooks were stymied in the early innings by Don Larsen, a pitcher who didn't use a windup, as the Yankees built up a 6 to 0 lead. But the Brooklyn hitters let loose a barrage that ousted Larsen and six other pitchers. Score: Brooklyn 13, New York 9.

Whitey Ford and newcomer Tom Sturdivant hurled the Yanks to victories in the next two games. This evened the Series at two-all.

Casey Stengel then called on Larsen to pitch the fifth game—once more against Sal Maglie. Maglie, for his part, pitched well enough to win most ball games. He gave up two runs on five hits, one of them a homer by Mickey Mantle.

But Maglie's performance didn't match Larsen's. By the middle of the ball game, the crowd woke up to the fact that Larsen might pitch a no-hit, no-run game. In every inning he retired three hitters in a row. Jackie Robinson was

The scoreboard tells the story of Don Larsen's perfect World Series game.

the only man who came close to getting a hit. In the third inning, Robinson slammed a vicious drive at third baseman Andy Carey. The ball glanced off Carey's glove and bounced to shortstop Gil McDougald, who threw Robinson out easily.

The tension kept mounting as the game rolled on. It reached its peak in the ninth inning.

Carl Furillo was the first hitter Larsen faced. He was put out on a fly. Roy Campanella, the next hitter, grounded out. A pinch-hitter, Dale Mitchell, moved to the plate in place of Sal Maglie.

The crowd hushed as Larsen pre-

pared to pitch. It was now obvious that all that stood between Larsen and a history-making record was the lone figure of Mitchell in a Brooklyn uniform.

"Ball one!" was the call on the first pitch.

Larsen rocked forward on the mound. His arm flashed downward.

"Stu-u-urike!"

Larsen kicked and fired again. Mitchell lashed at the ball and missed. It was strike two. Mitchell swung on the next pitch. This time he connected. The ball went foul.

The umpire threw a new ball into play. Larsen rubbed the slickness from

143

the cover. He glanced about the diamond, took a deep breath, and stepped on the rubber.

In the next second the ball whizzed past Mitchell and banged into the catcher's glove.

"Strike thur-e-eee-e!"

With that emphatic call Don Larsen became the first man to pitch a perfect game in World Series competition. In doing so he threw but 97 pitches.

The Yanks went on to win the Series in seven games.

The second classic performance occurred three years later in 1959. The Pittsburgh Pirates played a night game against the Milwaukee Braves in Milwaukee. The Pittsburgh pitcher was left-hander, Harvey "The Kitten" Haddix. His mound opponent was Lew Burdette. Haddix pitched flawlessly. Johnny Logan, the Braves' shortstop, was the only Milwaukee player to hit the ball with any force during the first nine innings. He drilled a shot to the right of the Pirate shortstop, Dick Schofield, but Schofield made a good play on the ball and threw Logan out easily.

To end the ninth, Haddix struck out Lew Burdette. Like Don Larsen, he had pitched a perfect game. No Walks. No hits. Twenty-seven outs in a row.

But the game was not over. Although Pittsburgh had gotten several hits off Burdette, the Pirates couldn't score. The game went into extra innings.

Haddix was still effective in the tenth. Three men up, three down. The scoreless tie remained, however, and Haddix went back to the hill in the eleventh. Again it was three up and three down.

Harvey Haddix in action the night he pitched 12 innings of perfect ball against Milwaukee.

There was no scoring in the eleventh and twelfth innings, or by the top of the thirteenth, even though Pittsburgh had collected 12 hits off Lew Burdette. This meant Haddix had to go to the mound at least once more.

The first man to face Haddix in the thirteenth was Felix Mantilla. He hit a routine ground ball to third baseman Don Hoak. Hoak fielded the ball cleanly and threw to first baseman Rocky Nelson. But the throw was wild! It hit Nelson on the foot and Mantilla, safe on the error, became the first Milwaukee runner.

The crowd buzzed excitedly as homer king Ed Mathews moved to the batter's box. But the Braves were taking no chances on a double play by the Pirates. Mathews got Mantilla to second on a sacrifice.

To set up another possible double play, Haddix purposely walked Hank Aaron. This brought Joe Adcock to the plate. Haddix wheeled the first pitch plateward. It was a ball. The second pitch was in the strike zone. But only for an instant, for the powerful Adcock swung and drove the ball deep to center field. Fleet Bill Virdon raced after the drive, made a desperate last-minute lunge at the ball. He couldn't get it. A Brave run scored and the game was over. Harvey Haddix had pitched perfect baseball for twelve innings, something no one had ever done before. Yet in one of baseball's most heartbreaking moments, Haddix lost his record-breaking game in the thirteenth.

Larsen and Haddix were the first men in over thirty years to pitch perfect games, yet both of them also set new records as well. Larsen's perfect nine innings came in World Series play. Haddix went beyond nine innings and pitched twelve perfectly before losing in the thirteenth. Certainly these were classic performances for any decade.

52. Hot Years for the Nationals

Though no one realized it at the time, the Pittsburgh Pirates signaled the beginning of the most remarkable period in National League history when they took the field to open the 1960 season.

The Pirates were called "an extraordinary hodge-podge" by one expert before the season and no one gave them much chance to win the pennant.

The Pirates, however, developed fine pitching, solid hitting, and a sound defense. Above all, the team never became discouraged. In early September, for example, the San Francisco Giants' left-hander Mike McCormick struck out 13 Pirates in a 6 to 3 victory. The next night Stan Williams of the Los Angeles Dodgers whipped the Pirates 5 to 2, again striking out 13 Pirates. Twenty-six strikeouts in two games!

But the Pirates bounced right back from these humiliating defeats, held off a fighting Milwaukee club, and won the National League pennant by seven games.

It was in the World Series with the

Yankees, however, that the Pirates demonstrated the sort of spirit that dominated National League play for the next several years.

The Pirates brought down the Yanks 6–4 in the opener at Forbes Field. Second baseman Bill Mazeroski drove a two-run homer over the scoreboard in the fourth inning to highlight the Pittsburgh attack. The New York *Times* noted Mazeroski was "never regarded as a long ball hitter."

Mickey Mantle led the Yanks to a 16–3 victory in the second game by bashing two tremendous drives—one 400 feet and the other 450 feet—out of the park. When the Series switched to Yankee Stadium, the Yanks ripped into the Pirates, scoring 10 runs as Whitey Ford held the Bucs scoreless on four hits.

The Pirates seemed undisturbed by the ferocity of the Yankee attack. They won the fourth game 3–2 and the fifth game 5–2. This gave Pittsburgh a 3 to 2 lead in games when the Series moved back to Pittsburgh for the finale.

After hitting the home run that gave Pittsburgh the 1960 World Series, a happy Bill Mazeroski cheerfully survives a champagne dousing from his fellow Pirates.

In the sixth game the Yankees broke loose with another amazing hitting spree. While Whitey Ford shut the Pirates out on seven hits, the Yanks clubbed five Pirate pitchers for 17 hits and 12 runs.

The seventh game was a battle all the way. First the Pirates were ahead, then the Yankees. By the end of the eighth inning, the Yanks were leading 7–4.

Gino Cimoli was the first man up for the Pirates in the bottom of the eighth. He singled to right field. Bill Virdon then hit a sharp grounder to shortstop Tony Kubek. It looked as if it might be the start of a routine double-play. To the horror of the crowd, the ball took a freak hop and hit Kubek in the Adam's apple. He dropped to the ground in agony. It was an important play. Instead of two outs and the bases empty, the Pirates now had runners on first and second with none out.

Play resumed after Kubek was taken from the field and rushed to a hospital. The next Pirate singled, bringing in Cimoli for a score. A sacrifice moved the runners to second and third. An infield hit scored another run and still left two men on the bases.

This brought Hal Smith, catcher, to the plate. He promptly drove the ball high over the left-field wall. The Pirates had scored five runs and now led 9–7. But the Yanks didn't give up. They scored two runs in the ninth to tie the score.

The crowd stirred restlessly as the teams changed places. It quieted as Bill Mazeroski moved to the batter's box to face Ralph Terry, the Yankees' fifth pitcher. In minutes the ball game was over. Mazeroski hit Terry's second pitch over the left-field wall.

That shot gave the Pirates a 10 to 9 victory and the first world championship in 35 years.

Like the Pirates of 1960, the Cincinnati Reds of 1961 were picked for the second division. But the Reds, powered by the bats of Vada Pinson and Frank Robinson and getting fine pitching from Joey Jay and Jim O'Toole, fooled all the experts by taking the flag four games in front of their nearest rival, the Los Angeles Dodgers. It was the first pennant in 21 years for the Reds and only the fourth since 1900.

Unlike the Pirates, however, the Reds were unable to add the World Championship to their laurels, dropping the Series in five games to the New York Yankees.

Naturally, the Pirates and Reds, by proving anyone might win in the National League in the 1960s, added a great deal of interest to the game. But it could not be compared to the attention the National League received in the years that followed. The first-division clubs staged a series of pennant races that, for sheer drama, were unprecedented in any similar time span.

In 1962, for instance, the Dodgers were either at the top of the standings or tied for the lead for 111 days. But the West Coast club was under constant challenge—especially from the San Francisco Giants. During a long and successful home stand on July 27, the Dodgers beat the Giants three straight. But when Los Angeles visited San Francisco in August, the Giants won three

straight. And when the season finally closed, the Giants and Dodgers were tied, setting the stage for the fourth play-off in the history of the League. In a best-of-three series, the Giants took the first game 8–0, lost the second 8–7, and won the third 6–4. In the World Series, however, the Giants bowed to the Yankees in seven games.

The following year, National League fans were treated to another sensational finish. For almost three-fourths of the season, five teams were bunched at the top of the standings. In midsummer the Dodgers began to pull away from the other four. But just as it seemed certain that they would win the pennant and make up for the loss of 1962, the St. Louis Cardinals put on a spectacular drive, winning 19 out of 20. At the end of this spurt, the Cards were one game behind the Dodgers and about to engage them in a three-game set at St. Louis. Johnny Podres whipped the Cards 3–1 on three hits in the opener, while teammate Sandy Koufax won the next game 4–0 on four hits. In the third game, the Cards fought bitterly for thirteen innings, but finally lost, 0–5.

From that point on, the Dodgers had little difficulty nailing down the championship. Nor did their winning ways stop there. They humiliated the Yankees in the 1963 World Series by taking four in a row by scores of 5–2, 4–1, 1–0, and 2–1.

For National League followers 1964 was even more exciting. And it provided one of professional baseball's strangest endings to a pennant chase.

The main interest revolved around the

Ken Boyer leaps into the crowd to make the last out in the fifth game of the 1964 World Series. Boyer's Cardinals won 5—2.

Philadelphia Phillies, a club that had finished last in 1961, seventh in 1962, and fourth in 1963. By the middle of the following year, it began to look as if the Phils would win their first pennant since 1950. On September 21, when the Phils took the field against the Cincinnati Reds, they led the League by six and a half games with but 12 games remaining. A championship seemed a certainty.

In the sixth inning, the Reds' Chico Ruiz stole home with two out and the Reds' best hitter, Frank Robinson, at bat. This odd play beat the Phillies. But an even more bizarre fate was in store

for them: they lost their next nine ball games!

While the Phillies were collapsing, the Cards, Reds, and Giants suddenly moved into contention. During the final three days of the season, the flag could have been won by any one of four teams. On the next-to-last day the Giants were eliminated. And on the last day the Cards and Reds were tied, with the Phils one game behind. The possibility of a three-way tie existed, but it ended when the Phillies whipped the Reds, 10–0, while the Cards won their last game, 11–5.

St. Louis pitcher Bob Gibson begins the final game of the 1964 Series. The Cards and Gibson beat the Yanks to win the championship.

The rousing finish by the Cardinals did not end all the drama, for the Red Birds then beat the Yankees in a seven-game World Series.

The Cards failed to play like champions in 1965, however. By July they were in seventh place, eight and a half games behind the front-running Dodgers. But if the Cardinals were out of the competition, four other teams were not. By late August, the Giants were trailing the Dodgers by only a game and a half; the Reds by 2; Milwaukee by 4, and Pittsburgh by 4½. During the last exciting month, however, only the Giants were in contention. But San Francisco was not up to the task and finished two games behind Los Angeles.

The Dodgers, featuring a "ping pong" attack and a fierce running game, went on to beat the new Minnesota Twins in the World Series in another seven-game set.

The "balance" between the top teams in the National League provided fierce pennant races that kept interest high. Most fans kept their attention on the standings, but in the meantime, baseball was changing again.

149

53. Reborn

After five teams moved to new cities during the 1950s, some fans thought the game would settle down again. But they were wrong.

Baseball was about to go through its biggest change since the turn of the century. The moving of teams to new areas had been tremendously successful. California, which was soon to have more people than any other state, had welcomed its new teams by providing new stadiums and record-breaking crowds. Milwaukee had been a good baseball city. The Baltimore and Kansas City teams were doing better than they had before they moved.

Baseball owners, who had been slow to change, now realized that there were other cities that would welcome major league teams. But why should one city lose a team so that another city could

have one? Why not create some new teams? Thus, shifting teams from one city to another paved the way for something else—expansion.

The American League took the initiative. When the 1961 season opened, the Washington Senators had moved to Minneapolis-St. Paul and become the Minnesota Twins. New teams were organized in Washington (the "new" Senators) and Los Angeles (the Angels). Thus the American League stretched to the West Coast for the first time.

The following year the National League also added two teams. One was placed in New York to make up for the desertion of the Dodgers and the Giants four years earlier. It became known as the Mets. The second team played in Houston, Texas, and started out as the Colt 45's. The name was soon changed

An Astrodome "Earthman" cleans the diamond before an exhibition game at Houston. Covered by a plastic dome, the unique, completely covered stadium is air-conditioned.

to the Astros and the team moved into the country's most remarkable stadium, the Astrodome. It was covered and air-conditioned to permit playing in any weather.

The expansion required the leagues to solve two problems. The first was, where would the new teams get their players? Both leagues solved the problem the same way. A special draft was organized in which the new teams could choose certain players from other teams in the league. Since the old teams could protect their better players, the new franchises in Washington, Los Angeles, New York and Houston started life with aging veterans and untried youngsters. Only the Angels climbed out of the second division in the first few years, finishing third in 1962. The others fought to stay out of the cellar.

A second problem was schedule. Since anyone could remember, the eight teams in each league played 154 games—22 against each other team in the league. With ten teams, the schedule would have to be changed. Club owners complained that there would be fewer chances each year for their teams to play traditional rivals. When the new 162-game schedule was adopted (18 games against each of nine other teams), the players grumbled that a long season had become too long.

And yet it seemed at first that both leagues would profit from the expansion. By the close of 1962, for example, total attendance went well over 21 million, setting a new all-time high. The National League drew 11,360,159 fans, setting a new major league record. Three years later the total reached more than 13.5 million. In the American League, however, attendance dropped by almost a million in 1963, steadied in 1964, then dropped again to 8,860,175 in 1965.

Something was lacking in American League play. It was competition. In 1962, for example, the Yankees won the pennant for the twelfth time in 14 years, finishing with a lead of five games. Although it was a narrow victory margin for the Yanks, there had been little doubt throughout the season that they would win. The next year the Yankees again captured the flag, this time by 10½ games. In 1964, when the Chicago White Sox ended the year only one game behind the Yanks, attendance picked up a little. But a year later the Minnesota Twins breezed to victory by seven games, and once again attendance fell off because of the lack of competition.

The American League officials took the lead again in seeking changes. They proposed dividing each League into two divisions. Under this plan, the winners of each division would meet in a play-off to decide who would represent the League in the World Series.

But the National League held back. They were doing well under the existing system and delayed a decision on division play.

Meanwhile, changes continued. In 1966, fans were shocked by the announcement that the Braves would move from Milwaukee to Atlanta. The town that had cheered baseball with its enthusiasm only nine years earlier had lost its team to a more promising territory.

No one doubted that Atlanta would be a good baseball city, but again a town had been unceremoniously "deserted" by a big league owner.

Also in 1966, the Los Angeles Angels moved into their own new stadium in Anaheim, California, about forty miles from the center of Los Angeles. They became the California Angels.

In 1968, before any action had been taken on the American League proposal for divisional play, another team changed cities and expansion was planned for 1969. The Kansas City Athletics moved to Oakland, California, giving the San Francisco area one team in each league. Then for 1969 new teams were established in Kansas City (the Royals) and Seattle (the Pilots). The team in Seattle lasted only one year before moving to Milwaukee as the Brewers, thus giving a happy ending to the story of the Wisconsin city's ups and downs with the big leagues.

The National League set a precedent by awarding one of its expansion teams to Montreal—the first major league team in Canada. Montreal had long had a top minor league club. The new team was called the Expos and was the only team to have its games broadcast in French. The second National League addition was the San Diego Padres.

Facing the 1969 season with twelve-team leagues, baseball's owners finally agreed on a completely revised organization. Each league would be divided into two six-team divisions. At the end of the season, the divisional winners would meet in a best three of five play-off to determine who would win the league title and play in the World Series. The National League, still doubtful, insisted that the new system be used on a one-year trial basis. The establishment of divisional "championship" play, however, proved so successful that it was continued.

Thus, after operating in the same mold for over 60 years, baseball had broken with the past. It had grown from 16 teams to 24, spread across the country and adopted a new play-off system. In structure, at least, the game was reborn.

54. Rise and Fall of the Yankees

Strangely enough, some of the problems of the American League were caused by the success of one team—the New York Yankees. The Yanks, originally known as the Highlanders, entered the league at its beginning in 1903 and didn't win their first pennant for 18 years.

Over the next 40 years, however, the Yankees won 25 pennants and 18 world championships. No other club in baseball even approaches that record.

The Yankees had enjoyed almost complete domination in the 1950s, winning the pennant eight times in ten tries, losing only in 1954 and 1959. On top of that, the Yankees whipped the top National League team in the World Series six times over the same period.

As the Yankees began the 1960s, they still dominated the league. Only Mickey Mantle, Yogi Berra and Whitey Ford remained from the remarkable teams that won five pennants and world championships between 1949 and 1953. But the club boasted new players, including Moose Skowron, Bobby Richardson, Tony Kubek, Elston Howard and Roger Maris.

In 1960 the Yankees made the poorest start in their history. Only right fielder Roger Maris and first baseman Moose Skowron seemed to hit the ball well. The pitching was both good and bad. Still, by August Casey Stengel was able to move the club into second place behind the Baltimore Orioles. The Orioles, made up of a few oldsters and several players barely old enough to shave, looked like sure winners.

But something unusual happened in Yankee Stadium as Stengel's team seemed to be losing a double-header to the Washington Senators.

In the second game Mickey Mantle came to bat with Roger Maris on first. There was one out. Mantle slapped a double-play grounder to the infield. Maris, realizing he was out at second, slid hard into second baseman Billy Gardner to hamper his throw to first and "save" Mantle.

Suddenly, the crowd let out a gasp, a roar, then a lusty round of boos. As Maris crashed into Gardner, Mantle stopped running!

"Quitter! Quitter!" the fans yelled at Mantle.

Had Mantle really quit?

Newsmen pressed Mantle for comment. But the slugger refused to say a word. The next day his bat spoke for him. He cracked two homers into the stands, each with a man on base, thereby driving in all the Yankee runs in a 4-3 victory.

From then on the Yankees picked up speed. They faltered once, dropping three games to the Orioles. But three weeks later they knocked the Orioles out of the race by sweeping a four-game series at Yankee Stadium. By the time it was over, Mickey Mantle, though injured, had hit 40 round-trippers to take the homer title for the fourth time.

153

"I was told my services were no longer desired," Casey tells the reporters.

"It's amazin' what he done," said Stengel. "And him a cripple playin' on one leg. He's been my most valuable player."

The Yankees surprised baseball by losing the World Series to the upstart Pittsburgh Pirates. But there were bigger surprises in store.

Shortly after the World Series, photographers and reporters jammed into a room of a New York hotel. They listened in amazement as Yankee owner Dan Topping read a prepared statement that Casey Stengel's contract would not be renewed. The Yankees, he said, had adopted an age-limit plan. Casey, at 70, was well beyond the limit.

Casey, grim of face, sat near Topping. For two hours he batted back the questions reporters threw at him.

"Were you fired, Casey?" one asked.

The lined face twitched. The old eyes glistened.

"Mr. Topping and Mr. Webb paid me

off in full and told me my services were no longer desired because they want to put in a youth movement as an advance way of keeping the club going," Casey said. "That was their excuse—the best they've got."

"Are you sad about leaving the Yanks, Case?"

"It's not a sad occasion," Casey replied with a straight face. "I look very happy. Ha, ha."

And so the manager with the best record in baseball history left baseball's most successful team.

The new Yankee manager was Ralph Houk, who had been in the Yankee organization for years. Fans wondered whether the New Yorkers could get along without Stengel.

In 1962 the Tigers provided the season's big surprise by quickly taking the lead in the American League. (They had been picked to finish deep in the second division.) They didn't yield first place until late July. And on September 1, when they traveled to New York for a three-game series with the Yanks, they were but a game and a half behind the first-place Bronx Bombers.

The Yankees, however, crushed Tiger dreams of landing in the World Series by taking the exciting and critical trio of contests by scores of 1–0, 7–2, and 8–5. These stunning victories seemed to spark the Yanks to even greater efforts. They won 13 more games in a row to increase their lead to 11½ games.

The Cincinnati Reds, also tabbed as a second-division team in the spring, upset the forecast by winning the National League flag. But the Reds were no match for the rampaging, hard-hitting Yankees in the World Series. They won only one out of five games. The scores were 2–0, 2–6, 3–2, 7–0 and 13–5.

The Yankees breezed to another pennant in 1962 and narrowly defeated the San Francisco Giants for their 20th world championship. During the season, the Yanks also faced competition in their home town for the first time since 1957. The New York Mets, a wildly inept group of ballplayers, set a major league record for losses in one season. But at least one Met was familiar to New Yorkers—the Met manager was Casey Stengel.

But the Yankees were unruffled. In 1963 they won the flag by 10½ games. The only sour note in the season was their staggering loss to the Dodgers in the World Series in four straight games. At the end of the season Ralph Houk became general manager and the new field manager was Yogi Berra.

The 1964 race was a close one. American League fans, who had nearly given up hope that the Yankees would one day be beaten, began wondering if the Yanks were beginning to slide. Still, after the last game of the season, the Yanks were on top for the fifth year in a row, leading the White Sox by one game.

The World Series against St. Louis was a cliff-hanger. Bob Gibson was the Cardinal hero, defeating the Yanks' Mel Stottlemeyer in the decisive seventh game. At the end of the Series, the Yanks and the Cards and the Mets played musical chairs with their managers. Johnny Keane announced he would not manage the Cardinals in 1965.

155

The Yankees announced that Berra had been released and Keane would be the new Yankee manager. Berra joined the Mets as a coach under Casey Stengel.

In 1965, under Johnny Keane, the Yankees began to fade, finishing 6th. Was it just bad luck? Keane left the club and Ralph Houk returned. Would the team be back on top in 1966? The answer was not long in coming. The club lost 10 of its first 11 games. It made a brief spurt, then slowly slid toward the cellar.

Mickey Mantle, bothered by injuries, had one of his poorest years, batting .288. But Mantle led the team in hitting. And the next highest average was only .266!

The pitching also fell apart. Mel Stottlemeyer had won 20 games in 1964 and was the best moundsman the Yankees had. In 1966, he lost 20. He also won 12, which was high for the entire staff. Adding to the pitching woes was Whitey Ford whose arm had finally failed. He

Yankee manager Yogi Berra gets doused with champagne after leading the Yanks to their last pennant of the 1960s.

pitched only 73 innings and won only two games.

When it was all over, the Yankees were last, 26½ games behind Baltimore, the new League champion. The next year, they did a little better, finishing 9th, 20 games behind first-place Boston. Few teams in baseball history went from top to bottom so rapidly. What went wrong?

With astonishing regularity, the Yankees had always filled the lineup with new stars whenever the old ones faded. Since the late 1930s, they had had an almost unbroken succession of great teams. Every year a few new stars appeared to replace the old ones.

But the supply of great players ran out in the mid-1960s. Slowly the Yanks had to get used to being just another team. It appeared that the greatest dynasty in baseball had come to an end.

55. New Heights

The 1960s produced two outstanding individual performances—one by a batter, the other by a base runner.

The batter was Yankee Roger Maris. In 1961 he and Mickey Mantle, began a march on Babe Ruth's season record of 60 homers, the most famous record in baseball. When it became obvious that this brawny pair might top Ruth's all-time mark, a hot argument broke out among ball fans and officials. Baseball Commissioner Ford Frick and American League President Joe Cronin took opposite sides. The question involved these points:

Ruth's record was set in a 154-game season. The Yankees in 1961 were playing 162 games. If Maris or Mantle hit 61 or more homers after the 154 game mark was passed, would Organized Baseball say Ruth's record had been broken?

"Yes!" said Cronin.

"No!" said Frick.

Frick's ruling prevailed. The fans seemed to agree.

As each day slipped by, however, it looked as though Ruth's record *might* be broken within the 154-game period. By game 134, Maris had 53 homers, Mantle 48. At that same point, Ruth had belted out 49.

On September 14, however, Mantle conceded the odds were against him. He had gone hitless in seven at-bats in a double-header against the Chicago White Sox.

"I can't make it, not even in 162 games," he said glumly. With 53 homers to his credit by that date, Mantle would have to hit seven in the six games that remained on the schedule.

Maris, too, seemed to be losing

Maris lifts his 61st homer of the season into the right field seats, thereby setting a record for a 162-game season.

ground. With 56 homers, he was one ahead of Ruth's pace for 148 games. But his last homer had been in game 142. Rugged Roger grimly continued swinging from the heels. In game 150, he hit his fifty-seventh homer; in game 151 his fifty-eighth. He now had tied the marks set by Jimmy Foxx in 1932 and Hank Greenberg in 1938.

Maris hit Number 59 during the 154th game. Ruth's record still stood. The fans settled back to see what Maris could do in the remaining games. Four games later he hit number 60. And on the last day of the season—before a roaring crowd at Yankee Stadium, Maris became the first player in major-league history to hit more than 60 homers "in a regular season."

While Maris set an individual record for homers in 1961, so did the players of both Leagues with 2,730. (The previous record had been established in 1956, when homers totaled 2,294.) Yet most people agreed that Maris had accomplished a prodigious feat. Even if he was no folk hero like Ruth, he deserved credit for his amazing performance.

The special base runner of the sixties was Dodger shortstop Maury Wills.

Wills, one of the smallest players in baseball, played his first full season in 1960. That year he totaled 50 stolen bases. Although he dropped to 35 in 1961, he still led the National League. A year later he began to steal bases as no one had in fifty years. Soon it appeared that he might challenge the record of 96 in one season, set by Ty Cobb in 1912.

As he neared Cobb's mark, a controversy arose similar to the one that preceded the Maris home-run feat of 1961. Would Wills be given credit for a record if he stole more than 96 bases in 162 games?

Commissioner Frick ruled that the record—if there was one—would have to be on the basis of 154 games. By the time Wills completed the 154th game, he had stolen 95 bases. But a check of the records showed that Cobb had achieved his total of 96 in a season of 156 games. (Two games had ended in a tie and were later replayed.) Wills, keeping the base paths hot, stole his 96th and 97th in the Dodgers' 156th game. By the close of the regular season, he had 100 stolen bases. During the play-off series with the Giants, he notched four more—three in the last game. The record of 104 stolen bases astonished baseball fans everywhere.

As the seasons rolled on, it did not seem possible that anyone would ever top records set by Maris and Wills. But then, fans felt the same way when Babe Ruth and Ty Cobb set the records that Maris and Wills broke.

Maury Wills slides safely into second base, stealing his 104th base of the season.

56. The Retirements

Old age, the enemy of every man, comes early in the life of a ball player—usually between 35 and 40.

As the 1959 season ended, it looked as though two of the finest players of all time—Ted Williams and Stan Musial—had reached the end of the road.

Williams had batted but .254, the lowest in his career. He was 41 years old. Musial, too, had his poorest season, hitting .255. He was 39 years old.

But Williams and Musial were men of pride, determined to end their careers on a better note. Both decided to play in 1960.

Williams got off to a fairly good start and batted close to or above .300 as the season moved along. On August 11, in a

game against Cleveland, The Splendid Splinter cracked two homers into the seats.

As the Red Sox flew to Baltimore, they broke training and drank a champagne toast to Williams. The two homers had moved him past Mel Ott, third among all-time homer hitters with 512.

Williams then decided that the September 28 game against the Baltimore Orioles would be his last. Although the weather was bad, a good crowd turned out to bid Williams farewell. When he came to bat for the last time in the eighth inning, the crowd stood and gave him a thundering ovation. Williams responded as only he knew how. He drove a 1–1 pitch into the Red Sox bull pen.

It was homer Number 521 for Williams, 13 fewer than second-place Jimmy Foxx. He hit .316 for 1960 and .345 for his career. He was named "Comeback Player of the Year" in the American League.

In 1969 Williams returned to baseball as manager of the Washington Senators (later the Texas Rangers).

For Musial it looked as if the decision to play in 1960 had been a mistake. By May he was only hitting .250 as the Cardinals dropped to the second division. Manager Solly Hemus had no choice but to bench his star. Musial remained on the bench for a month, until called on to replace an injured outfielder.

In September of 1960, Ted Williams slammed out his last homer for the Red Sox—the 521st of his career.

Stan Musial and Ted Williams meet in their last All Star Game in 1960.

By July Musial showed signs of recovering his form. Appearing as a pinch-hitter in an All-Star game, he blasted a long homer into the right-field stands. It brought the spectators roaring to their feet and kept them there for several minutes.

With that blow, Musial wrote some new facts into the record books. They were:

Most homers in All-Star games—Musial with 6.

Most total bases in All-Star games—Musial with 39.

Most at-bats in All-Star games—Musial with 57.

Most runs scored in All-Star games—Musial and Willie Mays of San Francisco with 11 each.

Musial's heroics didn't stop with the All-Star game. In August he batted at a .357 clip and had carried the Cards to within four games of the front-running Pirates. He finished the season with a .275 average, 17 homers, and 63 runs batted in.

It was such a remarkable recovery that he received the "Comeback Player of the Year" award in the National League. He decided to remain active and finally retired late in 1963.

As he ended his career in a game against the Cincinnati Reds, Musial collected two hits in three at-bats to pace the Cards to a 3–2 win. When the game was over, Musial had played in 3,026 games and batted 10,973 times. Credited with 3,630 hits, he had scored 475 homers, 177 triples and 725 doubles. His lifetime average was a remarkable .330.

Many other remarkable men retired before the 1960s ended:

*Early Wynn in 1963 after 23 years and an even 300 victories.

*Warren Spahn in 1965 after 21 years and 363 wins.

*Casey Stengel in July of 1965 after three and a half years with the hapless New York Mets and 56 years in baseball as a player, coach and manager.

*Whitey Ford in 1967 after 16 years and 236 wins.

*Mickey Mantle in 1969, after 18 years, 536 homers and three elections as the Most Valuable Player in the American League.

One of the famous retirements of the decade was a man who was hardly recognized when the 1960s began: Sandy Koufax.

57. Sandy

In baseball, as in other sports, a "super-star" is a player who stands head and shoulders above others in skill, courage and durability—a man who has much in common with the original Big Five of Ruth, Wagner, Cobb, Johnson and Mathewson.

As the 1960s progressed, it became clear that left-hander Sandy Koufax of the Los Angeles Dodgers was one of those who deserved to be identified as a super-star.

In a little more than 10 years in the majors, Koufax twice topped the National League in wins. On three occasions, he had the League's lowest earned run average, the true mark of great pitching.

Koufax' value to the Los Angeles Dodgers was amply demonstrated in 1962. That year the brilliant southpaw was at his best for the opening third of the season. In April, he equaled Bob Feller's record of eighteen strikeouts in one game, and on June 30th, he threw a no-hitter at the New York Mets. A short time later, however, he began to feel a strange numbness in his pitching hand. It started at the top of the index finger, spread to part of the palm and thumb. In mid-July, with his record at 14–5, Sandy was put on the disabled list.

As the season drew to a close, the erratic, stumbling Dodgers were tied by the Giants.

Although Koufax rejoined the club on September 21, in time to start the first game against the Giants in a play-off for the National League pennant, he lasted only two innings, and the Giants went on to win the pennant.

In 1963, Koufax was healthy again and had a 25–5 record and a sensational earned run average of 1.88. Eleven of his victories were shutouts, one a no-hitter over the Giants. He led the Dodgers to the pennant and then beat the Yankees twice in the Dodgers' four-game sweep of the World Series. In the first game, Sandy struck out 15 for a new Series record.

Although hampered by two serious injuries in 1964 and forced to withdraw before the close of the campaign, Koufax still managed to compile a 19–5 record and the League's lowest earned run average, which was 1.74. He also led National League pitchers in the number of shutouts, with seven.

Just prior to the start of 1965, Sandy became a victim of arthritis, a disease that cripples the joints. But his pitching arm responded to treatment and Sandy went on to enjoy probably his best season. On September 9th, for example, he pitched a perfect game as the Dodgers downed the Cubs, 1–0, at Los Angeles. That night he also became the first moundsman in baseball history to pitch four no-hitters during his career. The 29-year-old fireballer struck out 14, including the last six batters he faced.

On September 29, Koufax shut out the Reds on two hits as Maury Wills cracked out a three-run triple in a 5–0 Dodger victory. In this contest, Koufax struck out 13.

Two days later Koufax beat the Milwaukee Braves, 3–1. Once again he struck out 13, allowing only four hits. That victory gave the Dodgers the flag.

By the end of the regular season, Sandy had won 26, lost eight and set a major league record by striking out 382. His string of shutouts ran to eight and, as the Dodgers made their stretch drive, he gave up just one run in his last three starts.

The Dodgers lost their World Series opener against Minnesota, 8–6, with Don Drysdale pitching. Although Sandy pitched well the next day, he was behind, 2–1, when lifted for a pinch-hitter in the seventh. His removal caused one wag to remark: "Well, at least he's human."

Claude Osteen and Drysdale hurled the Dodgers to victory in the next two games and, with the Series tied at two all, Sandy won the fifth game, 7–0. He allowed but four hits.

The driving Twins again defeated the Dodgers in the sixth game, this time 5–1.

But Koufax took the mound for the final game and hurled the Dodgers to another World Championship.

Koufax and his mates had a hard time of it in 1966 as the Pirates, Dodgers and Giants ran neck-and-neck from mid-September on.

To avoid a tie with the Giants and also win the pennant, the Dodgers had

163

Dodger teammates congratulate Koufax after his perfect game against the Cubs.

to beat Philadelphia in their last game of the season. Koufax shut the Phils out, 6–0.

The Dodgers now had to face the Baltimore Orioles in the World Series. Paced by the hot bat and aggressive play of Frank Robinson—traded to the Orioles by the Cincinnati Reds during the winter months—Baltimore had gone into first place on June 14th, winning its first pennant with ease.

As in the Series the year before, the Dodgers' Don Drysdale pitched the opener and lost, 5–2.

For four innings of the second game, Koufax and his mound opponent, 20-year-old Jim Palmer, pitched one-hit

scoreless ball. In the top of the fifth, however, Willie Davis dropped two fly balls and threw wildly past third base to give the Orioles two unearned runs. A single scored another. In the sixth inning, Frank Robinson drove one of Sandy's pitches to the 390-foot sign in right center between Willie Davis and Ron Fairly. Either man could have caught the ball. By hesitating at the last moment, neither did and Robinson landed on third. A single brought him home. It was Sandy's last inning. While the Orioles picked up two more runs in the ninth, young Palmer shut out the Dodgers on four hits.

When the Series moved to Baltimore,

the Orioles won the next two games to notch their first World Championship.

On November 18th, Sandy called a press conference in Los Angeles. Seated before a cluster of microphones, bathed in television lights, and surrounded by newsmen and cameramen, Koufax, somewhat sadly, but firmly, announced his retirement from baseball.

He said he had made the decision because the arthritis that had afflicted his left elbow for two years might injure his arm permanently if he continued to pitch. The 30-year-old hurler left the game with a long and impressive string of records, some of which may never be equaled.

In 1972 he became the youngest man ever to be elected to the Hall of Fame. In his first year of eligibility he was overwhelmingly chosen at the age of 36.

Koufax pitches to Minnesota in the last game of the 1965 World Series.

58. Yaz and the Cinderella Team

With little question, the most spectacular pennant race in American League history took place in 1967. With just two days of the regular season left, a three-way tie was possible between one of two sets of teams and a two-way tie between one of four sets!

The three-way tie possibilities were: Minnesota-Detroit-Chicago and Boston-Detroit-Chicago. At the same time, a two-way tie could have developed be-

tween Minnesota-Detroit, Minnesota-Chicago, Boston-Detroit, or Boston-Chicago.

Although several players on these teams generated a great deal of excitement in the mad scramble for the pennant, one man proved a standout. He was 28-year-old Boston outfielder Carl Yastrzemski.

"Yaz" became the talk of the baseball world early in the season when it became clear that his hot bat and inspiring play were making a pennant contender of the Boston Red Sox. This was a startling development for the Red Sox. The Boston team had finished in the second division during the previous nine years and next to last in 1966.

Although he had never hit more than 20 home runs in a season, Yastrzemski, with some coaching from the old master, Ted Williams, became a sensational slugger overnight.

The left-hander's play was most dramatic during the fateful last two days of the season when the Red Sox, tied for second with Detroit and one game behind Minnesota, faced the Twins in Boston.

The situation was tense. Minnesota needed to win only one of the two games in order to take the flag and eliminate all tie possibilities. The Twins had beaten Boston in 11 of 16 games and now faced the Red Sox with their two best pitchers—Jim Kaat and Dean Chance.

Yastrzemski quickly upset the odds during the first game. In the fifth inning, he gave Boston a 2–1 lead with his second hit. In the eighth, a three-run homer proved the decisive blow in a 6–4 victory that kept the Red Sox pennant hopes alive.

As the final day dawned, a three-way tie still was possible among Minnesota, Detroit and Boston. But a Minnesota victory would mean a Minnesota championship.

By the sixth inning, Minnesota led 2–0, with Dean Chance, their 20-game winner, seemingly in control. Suddenly,

a bunt single and two line drives filled the bases for Boston as Yastrzemski stepped to the plate. On the second pitch, to a deafening roar from the crowd, he lashed a single to center to score the tying runs. Before the inning ended, the Sox scored three more.

But the Twins were not through. In the seventh, with one run in and a man on, Bob Allison drove a ball into the left-field corner for what seemed a sure double and a tie ball game. Yastrzemski raced to the ball, picked it up, whirled and made a powerful throw to second to nip Allison at second and halt the Minnesota threat.

Young Jim Lonborg, Boston's star hurler with 21 victories, kept the Twins at bay for the remainder of the game. When it was over, the score stood: Red Sox 5, Minnesota 3. Just as impressive as the score were the statistics compiled by Yastrzemski. In that vital two-game series, he had collected six hits in a row and seven in eight at-bats!

Still, the issue wasn't settled until a few hours later when the Tigers dropped the second game of a twin bill to the Angels, 8–5, after winning the opener, 6–4. The Tiger loss eliminated all possibility of a tie and gave the Red Sox their first pennant in 21 years.

Now, however, fans everywhere wondered how Boston would fare in the World Series against the St. Louis Cardinals, runaway winners of the National League. The majority felt the powerful Cardinals would crush the upstart Sox with ease.

By the end of the first series game, it looked as though the predictions would

Carl Yastrzemski takes a powerful swing during the 1967 Series. Yastrzemski's clutch hitting and fielding in the final days of the 1967 season helped spark the Red Sox on to their first pennant in 21 years.

certainly come true. St. Louis pitcher Bob Gibson, star of the 1964 Series, tamed the Sox 2–1 in the Boston opener as he struck out ten and gave up six hits.

But the Red Sox were not ready to give up. In game two, Lonborg pitched the second best game in Series history, topped only by the Don Larsen classic of 1956. He gave up just one hit—a double in the eighth to Julian Javier—shutting out the Cards, 5–0. Yastrzemski drove in four of the five Red Sox runs with two homers.

Seemingly undisturbed, the Cards won the third game, 5–2, on a homer by Mike Shannon and then took the fourth, 6–0, behind another brilliant pitching performance by Gibson.

To win the Series, the Cards had only to get by Lonborg in the fifth game, to be played in St. Louis. But Lonborg, with a paper horseshoe in his back pocket, was almost as effective as he had been in the second game. He gave up but three hits as the Sox whipped the Cards, 3–1.

Faced with elimination as the Series resumed in Boston, the Sox unleashed a barrage of homers by Rico Petrocelli, Yastrzemski and Reggie Smith. Their effective hitting paved the way to an 8–4 victory and evened the Series.

The final game pitted Gibson against Lonborg, but the anticipated pitching duel failed to develop. Lonborg, trying to pitch with only two days' rest, lost his power by the middle of the game. Gibson, on the other hand, was as strong as ever after three days' rest. With Javier bashing a three-run homer in the sixth and Brock collecting two hits and stealing three bases, the Cards ground their way to a 7–2 victory and their eighth World Championship.

The Red Sox missed the biggest prize by one game. But they had come up from the last place, amazing the baseball world.

As for Yastrzemski, his season average of .326 and 121 runs-batted-in was the best in the American League. He also tied Harmon Killebrew with 44 homers and became the 11th man to win the Triple Crown. In addition, he won the League's Most Valuable Player award.

Thus, the year 1967 belonged to the "Cinderella" team and a man called Yaz.

59. The Year of the Pitcher

In the history of baseball there have been periods when batters dominated the game and other periods when the pitchers ruled. In 1961, the year that Roger Maris hit 61 home runs, the batters seemed clearly in charge. But as the decade came to a close, the emphasis was on pitching.

In 1968 the power of the pitchers reached its height. Scores of statistics showed clearly that the pitchers were dominating the hitters. The combined batting average for both leagues, for instance, was .236, the lowest ever recorded. Home runs dropped to 1,994 from a high of nearly 3,000 in 1962. And only in 1908 were fewer runs scored per game.

Individual performances also underlined the new power of the pitcher. Bob Gibson, in leading the St. Louis Cardinals to victory in the National League, posted an earned run average of 1.12, a National League record. The Detroit Tigers' Denny McLain paced his team to the American League crown with a 31–6 record. He was the first man since Dizzy Dean in 1934 to win thirty games in a season.

Two other remarkable performances kept the spotlight on pitching. On May 8, Jim "Catfish" Hunter hurled the first perfect game in the American League in 46 seasons as Oakland whipped Minnesota 4–0. In May and early June, Don Drysdale of the Dodgers established two more significant records: he hurled six straight shutouts and notched 58⅔ scoreless innings to top a mark set by Walter Johnson in 1913.

Fans' interest in pitching reached a climax with the World Series. The opening game in St. Louis, featuring Bob Gibson against Denny McLain, was billed as the "pitchers' battle of the century." McLain proved disappointing, but Gibson set a new Series record by striking out 17 men, and the Cards won 4–0.

Although Gibson won the fourth game and McLain kept the Tigers alive by winning the sixth, another Tiger pitcher named Mickey Lolich stole the show. He won the second and fifth games and was picked to pitch against Gibson in the decisive seventh game.

The two dueled evenly for six innings. But in the seventh Gibson weakened and gave up three runs. Both teams scored

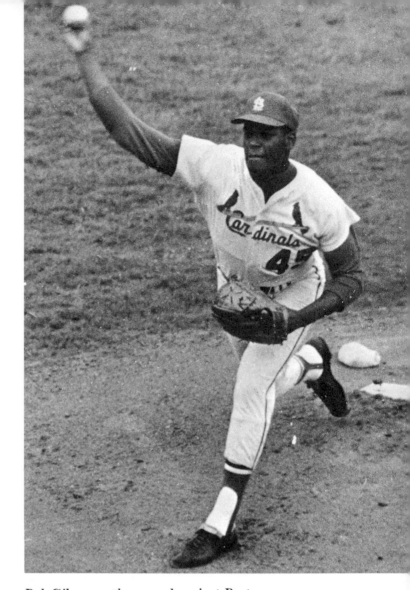

Bob Gibson on the mound against Boston.

By June of 1968 Don Drysdale had hurled 6 straight shutouts and notched 58⅔ scoreless innings.

Mickey Lolich, the surprise pitching hero of the World Series, after winning the final game.

a run in the ninth, but Lolich was the hero and the Tigers were world champions.

After the season, called "the Year of the Pitcher," there was a clamor for rule changes to restore a better balance between pitchers and batters. After much argument, baseball owners agreed to make the strike zone smaller and to lower the pitcher's mound. This, they hoped, would put the classic tug-of-war between hitter and pitcher on a more even footing.

The dispute over new pitching restrictions was only one of many disputes that disturbed baseball in the winter between the 1968 and 1969 seasons. The two leagues had agreed that each would ex-

pand to twelve teams for the 1969 season but disagreed violently about schedule changes. The National League finally agreed to try the two-division plan favored by the American League and it became the new schedule for the years to come.

Shortly after the Series, the Players' Association announced that no contracts for the new season would be signed unless owners agreed to changes in the player pension plan. Only a few weeks before, the leagues' umpires had almost walked out on strike just before the World Series.

The Commissioner of Baseball, Gen. William D. Eckert, who had been appointed in 1965, was one victim of the unrest. Even though the owners had been partly responsible for the troubles, they blamed them on Eckert and fired him.

On December 21 the owners met to choose a new commissioner. They were in session for 19 hours and cast 19 ballots, but could not agree on a candidate. Thus baseball faced the New Year without a commissioner, threatened with strikes by players and umpires and unsure about its new twelve-team schedule. It looked as if baseball was in for some bad times.

On February 4th, however, the owners suddenly pulled themselves together and elected Bowie Kuhn, a 42-year-old lawyer familiar with baseball affairs, as the game's new commissioner. Three weeks later the contract dispute with the players was settled.

On that hopeful note spring training began and the 1969 season approached.

60. The Amazin' Mets

Although there was a special kind of love in the heart of every New York Met rooter during the team's first seven years in the National League, it was often mixed with rage, contempt, anguish, pity, frustration or laughter. But, on October 16, 1969, the affections of Met followers winged to unprecedented heights and with this change came two new emotions—awe and pride.

Naturally, it was the Mets' performance that caused such a range of reaction. For even in so short a lifetime, the Mets managed to play the poorest, zaniest and, finally, most exciting and heroic brand of baseball ever witnessed in the majors.

During their first seven seasons, for example, the Mets lost every opening day game, finished last five times and next to last twice. And in seven 162-game seasons, the club averaged more than 100 defeats a year.

Opening day of 1969 followed the usual pattern. But the Mets' reputation as the sorriest team in baseball began to change in June, when their won-lost average reached .500. Although the feat of winning as many games as they lost was actually a milestone, this Met achievement was soon forgotten. In mid-August—while 9½ games behind the Chicago Cubs—the Mets began a drive that enabled them to clinch the East Division title by September 24. To eliminate the Cubs, a team that held first place for 155 consecutive days, the

Mets won 35 of 45 games during this home-stretch run.

Then they astonished everyone by defeating the powerful Atlanta Braves—winners of the West Division—three straight by scores of 9–5, 2–0 and 7–4 in a three-out-of-five series. Meanwhile, the Baltimore Orioles whipped the Minnesota Twins in American League division play-offs, also in three consecutive games.

Baseball fans everywhere, it seemed, were now asking the same question: could the improbable Mets—youngest team in the majors—actually go on and capture the World Series title?

Donn Clendenon hammers out another homer, this time in the fourth Series game.

For the Mets, the dream of such a possibility received a rude jolt in the very first game. Baltimore southpaw Mike Cuellar polished off the New Yorkers, 4–1, on six hits. The Baltimore victory also ended an 11-game winning streak for Tom Seaver, the Mets' best pitcher.

But Jerry Koosman, with ninth-inning help from Ron Taylor, downed the Orioles, 2–1, in the second game, thereby evening the record.

When the teams moved from Baltimore to New York for game three, the term "Met Magic" became common on sports pages. Met outfielder Tom Agee gave meaning to the term by bashing a lead-off homer over the center-field wall and turning back at least five Baltimore runs with spectacular catches in the fourth and seventh innings. Pitchers Gary Gentry and Nolan Ryan held the Orioles to four hits as the Mets crushed their rivals, 5–0.

A homer by Donn Clendenon in the second inning of the fourth game got the Mets off to another head start. Tom Seaver gave up two hits in the third, but held Baltimore scoreless. He then retired 19 of the next 20 batters he faced.

For a while it looked as if the Mets' 1–0 lead might disappear when Oriole Frank Robinson singled with one out in the top of the ninth and moved to third on another single by John Powell. A single by Brooks Robinson, the next batter, could score one run and move what might be the winning run to third.

Brooks drilled a shot to right field. It looked as if it would drop in for a hit—but no! Ron Swoboda made a diving,

tumbling catch just before the ball hit the ground. Although Frank Robinson scored after this bit of "Met Magic," Seaver snuffed out the next batter and the lead run "died" on base.

With the score tied at 1–1 in the bottom of the tenth, Jerry Grote stroked what seemed a routine fly ball to Oriole outfielder Don Buford. To the roaring amazement of the huge Shea Stadium crowd, Buford lost the ball in the sun. It dropped, untouched, for a freak double. As the stadium quieted down, the Orioles deliberately walked Al Weiss. With the left-handed J.C. Martin at bat, the Orioles replaced right-handed pitcher Dick Hall with left-hander Pete Richert. It was now clear to the thousands in the ball park and the millions watching the game on television that Martin had but one thing to do: bunt!

Martin didn't fail. He dropped a beauty 10 feet from the plate and set off for first as Rod Gaspar, running for Grote, headed for third. Richert raced off the mound, pounced on the ball, whirled and fired to first. But the ball hit Martin and caromed into right field as Gaspar flew around third and scored! (The Orioles claimed—and later pictures showed them to be correct—that Martin illegally interfered with Richert's throw but the umpires said no.)

In the fifth game, the Orioles, stung by the humiliation of three straight defeats, jumped on the Mets' Jerry Koosman for three runs in the third inning. But the Mets, with the world championship at their fingertips, would not give up.

Koosman retired 19 of the next 21

batters. Donn Clendenon hit a two-run homer in the sixth and Al Weis hit one in the seventh to tie the score at 3–3. As their fans roared themselves hoarse, the Mets added two more in the eighth, chalking up a victory that did, indeed, seem magical.

The fantastic Met victory brought a happy ending to a season of turmoil and provided the appropriate excitement for organized baseball's 100th anniversary year. The game might still have serious problems to be solved, but the Mets proved once more that heroism on the field brought new fans and admirers to the national pastime.

61. The Robber

The "magic" that was so much a part of the New York Mets' style of play in 1969 failed them in 1970—especially in September when they needed it most.

The Mets were in a three-way battle with the Pirates and the Cubs as the season drew to a close. On successive weekends, the New Yorkers met the Pirates seven times. They lost six of the games, five of them by one run. They also hit into 16 double plays and left 66 runners on base. As a result, the Pirates clinched the Eastern Division championship.

Cincinnati had long since made a runaway of the race in the National League Western Division, so they faced the Pirates in the post-season playoffs. Meanwhile, Baltimore and Minnesota had been victorious in their divisions and they met in the American League playoffs.

Surprisingly, both the Reds and the Orioles won three straight games against their playoff opponents to qualify for the World Series. The stage now seemed set for a classic battle between power and pitching. Cincinnati, with 191 home runs, had the most powerful attack in the National League. The Orioles, on the other hand, boasted the finest pitching in the American League. Dave McNally, Mike Cuellar and Jim Palmer had all won 20 or more games.

But the Series gave the fans a surprise. It was the play of the Orioles' third baseman, Brooks Robinson, that stole the show.

Robinson began his one-man act in the first inning of the first game. The Reds had jumped to a 1–0 lead and had two men on with two out when Bernie Carbo came to bat. Carbo drilled a line drive toward third. It looked as if the Reds would score again, but Robinson snagged the ball and the inning was over.

Robinson added his bat to the Oriole

cause in the 7th inning by cracking out a home run that meant a 4-3 victory for pitcher Jim Palmer and the Orioles.

In the second game, the Reds again got off to a quick start, scoring three runs in the early innings. Their center fielder, Bob Tolan, homered in the third to put his team ahead 4–0. The next hitter walked. Then Lee May promptly hit a hard grounder down the third base line. Again it looked like trouble for the Orioles. But again Robinson cut the ball off—this time with a spectacular back-hand stop, a pivot and a fine throw to second to start a double play.

The Orioles picked up one run in the fourth inning on a home run by first baseman Boog Powell and five more in the fifth, giving them a 6-4 lead. The hit that put the Orioles ahead was off the bat of Brooks Robinson. Three Baltimore relief pitchers protected the lead and the Orioles won the game 6–5.

The Reds began the third game with another serious threat. Right fielder Pete Rose singled in the first; then Bob Tolan singled and Tony Perez ran the count to two balls and no strikes. But Perez made the mistake of hitting a high hopper toward Brooks Robinson. Robinson took the ball behind third, stepped on the bag for one out, and fired the ball to first to complete a snappy double play. Then Johnny Bench, the National League's Most Valuable Player, lashed a line drive toward third. With a flick of his glove, Robinson speared the ball for out number three.

When the Orioles went to bat, they loaded the bases with two out in the first. The Reds' pitcher, Tony Cloninger,

needed to retire only one more batter to end the inning. But the batter was Brooks Robinson. He slapped Cloninger's third pitch into right center field for a double to get the Orioles off to a two-run lead.

With the Orioles leading 4–1 in the sixth inning, Robinson again doubled. Soon the bases were loaded and pitcher Dave McNally hit a grand slam homer to make the score 8–1.

In the next inning Johnny Bench slammed another shot at third. Robinson made a dive to his left and caught the ball inches from the ground. Although the Reds scored twice in the inning, the Orioles won their third game in a row, by a score of 9–3.

A three-run homer by Lee May gave the Reds a 6–5 win in the fourth game and prevented the Orioles from sweeping the Series. But even in defeat, Robinson excelled, hitting a home run and three singles.

In the fifth game, won by the Orioles 9–3, Robinson contributed a single to Baltimore's 15-hit attack and robbed Bench of another hit—this time by diving to his right to make a back-handed catch.

To no one's surprise, Robinson was voted the most valuable player of the Series. Hitting safely in every game, he had driven in six runs, scored five, and compiled an average of .429. In all, he collected two homers, two doubles and five singles.

Still, it was his defensive work that was most impressive. Time and again, his quick glove had brought Cincinnati's Big Red Machine to a halt just when it

Brooks Robinson dives after a ground ball hit by Lee May in the second game of the 1970 World Series. He recovered in time to start a double play.

threatened to break loose.

As always, there were events off the diamond that attracted attention in 1970. St. Louis outfielder Curt Flood had been traded to the Phillies after 1969 but had refused to play. Instead, he took baseball to court. He contended that the reserve clause, which makes a player the property of one team, amounted to "slavery." In 1971 he signed to play for the Washington Senators, but shortly after the season opened he quit baseball for the second time. He also continued his suit against baseball, and the U.S. Supreme Court agreed to hear his case.

For most fans, court cases were less interesting than the achievements of players like Brooks Robinson, whose sensational play had stolen the World Series for Baltimore.

62. The Last Pirate

The Baltimore Orioles, with the best pitching in baseball, did the predictable in 1971. They won their third American League pennant in a row and their fourth in six years.

The Orioles faced only one serious obstacle as they rolled toward the championship and that was a tall, slender, left-handed pitcher who wore the uniform of the Oakland Athletics and bore the unusual name of Vida Blue.

Blue, only 22 and a freshman in the majors, seemed unbeatable at times. During the first half of the season, he compiled a 17–2 record. Although he slipped a little in the second half, he still wound up winning 24 and losing 8. His earned run average was 1.82, the best in the League. He won the Cy Young award as best pitcher in the league and was named the Most Valuable Player.

In regular season play, Blue had beaten the Orioles twice with ease. Thus, when the Orioles and A's captured the East and West division titles, it became clear that Baltimore would have to beat Vida Blue in the play-offs if they hoped to win the League title.

For the first six innings of the opening play-off game in Baltimore, Blue continued his mastery of the Orioles as the A's built a 3–1 lead. But he gave up a walk, two singles and a double with two outs in the seventh. Suddenly the Birds were ahead 5–3 and Blue was lifted from the game.

Blue's loss seemed to take all the heart out of the A's. The Orioles won the next two games to sweep the divisional play-off for the third year in a row.

In the National League the Pittsburgh Pirates easily captured the National League East title for the second year in a row. But the race in the West was another matter. The San Francisco Giants took the Division lead in April but by the last day of the season their lead over the Dodgers had shrunk to one game.

In that last game, Juan Marichal held San Diego to five hits and the great Willie Mays, now 40 years old, slammed a 410-foot home run. The Giants won 5–1 and clinched the West title.

But with every key player suffering one kind of injury or another, the Giants were no match for the eager Pirates, losing the play-offs in four games.

Now the stage was set for baseball's 68th World Series—the Pirates vs. the Orioles. The Orioles had four pitchers who had won 20 or more games during the season and their pitching edge made them a heavy favorite when the Series opened in Baltimore.

The Orioles slapped the Pirates down 5–3 in the first game. Although he got off to a shaky start, Baltimore's Dave McNally (21–5) held the Bucs to three hits.

Baltimore continued to dominate Pittsburgh in the second game, crushing the Pirates 11–3 behind Jim Palmer (20–9). For Baltimore, the hero of this game was the hero of the 1970 World Series, Brooks Robinson.

He drove in three runs with three singles and made a spectacular, diving play on a ground ball in the eighth to rob catcher Manny Sanguillen of a hit.

Now the Series shifted to Pittsburgh, but the Pirates' chances seemed dim indeed. But the Pirates were not intimidated by the odds. They beat the Orioles 5–1 as Steve Blass outpitched Mike Cuellar (20–9). The biggest blow for Pittsburgh was a homer by first baseman Bob Robertson in the seventh inning with two on and none out. (Ironically, Robertson had been ordered to bunt, but missed the sign.)

Game four was the first night game in World Series history. A record television audience of over 63 million watched the Pirates nose out Baltimore 4–3 behind the four-hit pitching of Luke Walker and young Bruce Kison. Again Clemente was the top Pirate hitter, getting three of the Pirates' 13 hits in the rout of Baltimore's fourth 20-game winner, Pat Dobson, and three other hurlers.

Brimming with confidence, the Bucs made it three straight the following day as Nelson Briles beat Dave McNally, shutting the Orioles out 4–0 on a brilliant two-hitter.

Now the Series stood 3 games to 2 in favor of Pittsburgh. Should the Bucs win the next one, they would become the first team to win four games in a row after dropping the first two.

The sixth game contained just about all the drama and excitement one can expect from any sporting event. Roberto Clemente brought the crowd to its feet in the very first inning when he blasted a triple to left-center off Jim Palmer. But his teammates left him on third.

In the second inning, however, the

Sensational Vida Blue won 24 games in his first full season with Oakland.

aggressive Pirates scored when Al Oliver doubled and was singled home by Bob Robertson. Clemente then made it 2–0 by slashing a drive over the right-field wall—his 11th hit in 23 at-bats.

But the Orioles were not giving up. They scored once in the sixth and again in the seventh to tie the game at 2-all— a tie that held through the eighth and ninth.

In the Oriole 10th, Frank Robinson

walked with one out. A single to center sent him streaking for third. He made a headlong dive for the bag and barely beat the throw from the outfield.

Brooks Robinson came to the plate. He looped the ball to shallow left-center. Frank Robinson tagged up after the catch, then tore home in another race with the ball. As catcher Manny Sanguillen reached for the ball on the first bounce, Robinson hit the dirt on his side, crashing into the Pirate catcher and across the plate. Frank had scored and the Orioles had won!

In the decisive seventh game Steve Blass started for Pittsburgh and Mike Cuellar for Baltimore. They provided more pressure baseball at its best.

Blass gave up two walks and a single in the first four innings. But Cuellar was even·tougher. He retired the first 11 men in order. He then faced Clemente—the one Pirate hitter the Orioles had not been able to tame. Clemente promptly bashed the ball over the fence

in left-center for a 1–0 Pirate lead. It was Roberto's 12th hit in 27 at-bats.

In the eighth inning Pittsburgh made it 2–0 when Stargell singled and came home on a double by Jose Pagan.

In the bottom of the eighth, the Orioles put the tying runs on second and third on two singles and a sacrifice. One run scored on a fielder's choice. But the inning ended on a ground ball.

The Pirates failed to score in the ninth and now the Orioles came to bat. Blass, who had given up only four hits, was tougher than ever.

Powell grounded out. Frank Robinson popped up. Rettenmund grounded out.

The Pirates were champs!

The astonishing climax, coming after defeats in the first two games, proved again that the Pirates were tough customers in the World Series. They had won four out of six, and always in the full seven games. A World Championship match with Pittsburgh is never over until the last Pirate is "out."

Roberto Clemente, one of baseball's great hitters, rounds third on a home run against Baltimore in the World Series.

63. An Unusual Year

Baseball was never more unpredictable than in 1972. On Opening Day, for example, no games were played. The team owners were faced with the first serious players' strike since the Brotherhood Revolt of 1890. The strike was called by the Players' Association when the owners refused to increase the player pension fund by one million dollars.

A compromise finally ended the walkout, but only after 13 playing dates had been lost. Many fans, disgusted with both sides of the dispute, lost interest in baseball—at least temporarily.

Soon after the season finally got underway, fans were jolted again. Willie Mays, who had spent 21 great years with the Giants, had been traded to the New York Mets. In his first game as a Met he hit a homer to beat the Giants 5–4. But Willie was aging, and he had a poor season.

In the pennant races, the Pittsburgh Pirates and the Cincinnati Reds quickly took the lead in their division of the National League, rolling finally to easy victories. The Oakland Athletics were soon far ahead in the American League West.

But in the AL East, the favored Baltimore Orioles failed to play up to expectations. They dropped into a four-way race with Detroit, Boston and New York. By the last week of the season, only Detroit and Boston were left. The Tigers came out victorious and went on to meet Oakland in the play-off for the pennant.

Willie Mays, one of the game's great sluggers, tees off for his new team, the New York Mets.

In both leagues, the play-offs went the full five games for the first time. In the American League, the surprising A's took the final game from the Tigers 2–1, but the victory was costly. Their star, Reggie Jackson, was injured and would not play in the World Series.

In the deciding fifth game of the National League play-offs, the Pirates were leading Cincinnati going into the bottom of the ninth. But Reds' catcher Johnny Bench (who was later named the league's Most Valuable Player) homered to tie the score. Moments later, pinch-runner George Foster scored the winning run on a wild pitch by Pirate pitcher Bob Moose. The final score: 4–3.

179

The solid Reds were favored to win the 69th World Series. But the flamboyant A's, who wore colorful green and gold uniforms and sported long hair and mustaches, won the opener in Cincinnati. Catcher Gene Tenace, a lowly .225 hitter during the regular season, hit home runs in his first and second times at bat, driving in all of the A's runs in a 3–2 triumph.

In the second game, Oakland's Joe Rudi was the hero, hitting a homer in the third inning and making a game-saving catch in the bottom of the ninth. The A's won 2–1.

The Reds' prospects for a World Championship looked poor indeed. They had lost the first two games at home and now faced three games in Oakland. The records showed that no team in this situation had ever come back to win.

Still, the Reds' hopes rose when they took the third game with a single "gift" run. Tony Perez, trying to score from second on a single, slipped and fell halfway between third and home. But the A's cut-off man, Bert Campaneris, had his back to Perez. Before Campy could throw home, Perez had scrambled to his feet and crossed the plate, giving the Reds a 1–0 victory.

In the fourth game, Oakland's unlikely hero, Gene Tenace, hit a third homer. Then in the ninth inning, with the Reds leading 2–1, Tenace hit one of three singles, and the A's scored two runs to win the game 3–2. Now Oakland really had the upper hand, with a three-games-to-one advantage.

Oakland fans came out for the fifth game hoping to see the A's bring the

An unlikely slugger, Oakland's Gene Tenace, slams a home run in the first game of the World Series. He hit four in the Series, tying a record held by Babe Ruth, Lou Gehrig and others.

first World Championship to Northern California. Their hopes were almost rewarded when Gene Tenace hit a three-run homer in the second inning to put the A's ahead. But the Reds' big hitters —Pete Rose, Joe Morgan and Bobby Tolan—came around for the first time in the Series and brought the Reds a 5-4 win.

The contest returned to Cincinnati, and MVP Johnny Bench kept the Reds' attack going. He homered off Oakland's Vida Blue and the Reds went on to take an easy 8-1 victory. It was the first game of the Series to be decided by more than one run.

Both teams had won two games in enemy territory and only one at home. Now the question was whether the A's could win one more in Cincinnati. They scored a run in the first inning and held their lead until the fifth, when the Reds tied it up. Then in the sixth, amazing Gene Tenace drove in a run with a double and scored a moment later on Sal Bando's double. Now it was 3-1.

In the eighth the Reds made one more mighty effort. Rose and Morgan got on base. Then with one out, Johnny Bench was walked. Now it seemed that the Reds could break the game open.

But relief pitcher Rollie Fingers got the next two batters to fly out (one run scored after the first catch) to end the inning. Fingers held on in the ninth and the A's had done it, winning the seventh game 3-2.

The excitement and controversy of the season were muted by the deaths of three remarkable baseball men. In April,

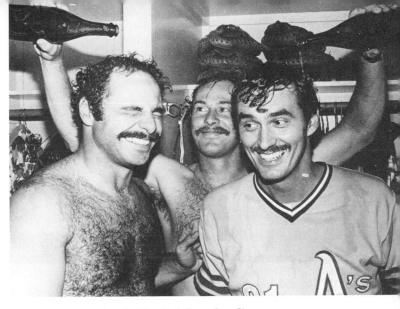

Three mustachioed A's, Sal Bando, Gene Tenace and Dal Maxville, celebrate their World Series victory.

Gil Hodges, manager of the Amazing Mets and former Brooklyn Dodger star, died suddenly. He was replaced as Met manager by Yogi Berra.

In October, another Dodger great, Jackie Robinson, was a guest at the World Series to commemorate the 25th anniversary of his breaking the color line in baseball. A few weeks later he died. Concerned to the end that blacks have an equal chance, Robinson had recently reminded baseball that a black manager in the majors was long overdue.

On the last day of 1972, Roberto Clemente died in an airplane crash. Clemente was on a cargo plane carrying relief supplies from Puerto Rico to earthquake victims in Nicaragua.

Continuing the trend of player-owner disagreements, Curt Flood's suit against baseball ended when the Supreme Court ruled in favor of the owners. The "reserve clause" remained in dispute, however, threatening to bring the game to a screeching halt when the new season began.

181

64. Alive and Well in '73

Baseball, long America's favorite pastime, slipped badly in popularity during the 1960s. Expansion, shifting franchises and one-sided pennant races all contributed to the decline. But the introduction of East-West division play gave the sport a big boost in the '70s.

More teams had a chance to win then, since there were four big races instead of two. And post-season play included two exciting playoffs in addition to the World Series itself.

By late September 1973, three of the four division races had been decided. Baltimore and Oakland had finished first in the American League, and Cincinnati ran away from the National League West with the best won–lost record in the majors.

But in the National East, an amazing see-saw battle was in progress. Until the last few days of the season, five teams—St. Louis, Pittsburgh, Montreal, Chicago and New York—all had a crack at the title. All five teams were struggling to stay above a .500 won–lost percentage, which led someone to dub the division the "National League Least." Still, one of the teams had to win.

The division crown finally went to the New York Mets, the most unlikely club of all. From last place in late August, the Mets put on an amazing surge, winning 23 of their last 32 games—and winning the title on the last day with the worst record in history.

It seemed unlikely that the Mets could survive the National League playoffs against the powerful Reds.

As expected, the Reds downed the Mets in the opener. Met ace Tom Seaver turned in an impressive 13-strikeout performance, but a ninth-inning homer by Johnny Bench gave Cincinnati a 2–1 victory. In game two the Mets came back behind the superb pitching of Jon Matlack who shut out the Big Red Machine, 5–0.

The weak-hitting New Yorkers surprised the Reds in game three. Two home runs by Rusty Staub contributed to a 9–2 rout of the Reds. But the Mets' hot hitting was only part of the day's excitement. In the fifth inning Cincinnati's Pete Rose tore into Met shortstop Bud Harrelson to break up a double play. In a flash, all 50 players of both teams were throwing punches on the field. When Rose took his position in left field an inning later, Met fans pelted him with empty bottles and other trash. Only pleas from a delegation of Mets prevented a full-scale riot—and forfeiture of the game.

In game four the teams played twelve innings before a homer by Rose gave Cincinnati a 2–1 victory and tied the Series at two all. But in the fifth and final game the Mets subdued the Reds 7–2. The Mets—amazing once again—had won the pennant.

Meanwhile, in the American League an equally fierce battle was taking place between the Baltimore Orioles and the Oakland Athletics.

Baltimore's pitching star Jim Palmer won the first game with a superb five-hitter. But the Athletics bounced back

Cincinnati's Pete Rose crashes into Met shortstop Bud Harrelson during the National League playoffs. Wayne Garrett (left) rushed to Bud's rescue, and seconds later players from both teams were fighting on the field.

with a victory in the second game.

Oakland won the third game when Bert Campaneris homered in the bottom of the eleventh to end a brilliant pitching duel between Baltimore's Mike Cuellar and Oakland's Ken Holtzman. But the Orioles evened it up again by winning the fourth game 5–4.

Once again the ticket to the World Series was riding on the crucial fifth game. Behind the five-hit pitching of Jim "Catfish" Hunter, the A's took a 3–0 victory—and won their second pennant in a row.

So powerful Oakland and the unlikely Mets were the World Series teams. Playing in their home park, Holtzman and the A's squeezed out a 2–1 win over Matlack in the first game.

In the second game the score was 0–0 after nine innings. In the tenth, Met Bud Harrelson got to third with one out. Felix Millan then flied out to short left. Harrelson sprinted home after the catch and twisted by A's catcher Ray Fosse. But umpire Augie Donatelli—in a highly disputed call—ruled that Harrelson had been tagged.

The 6–6 deadlock continued until the twelfth inning, when the Mets scored four runs (with a little help from Oakland's second baseman Mike Andrews, who comitted two errors). Final score: New York 10, Oakland 7. The game lasted more than four hours, and many believed that New York had actually won it twice.

Game three was another long one, but this time the A's sent Seaver to the shower, beating the Mets 2–1 in eleven innings. The Mets evened the Series by crushing Oakland, 6–1, and then went ahead in the fifth game with a 2–0 win.

In game six the A's Reggie Jackson and Catfish Hunter combined their talents to down the Mets, 3–1, and evened the Series at three games apiece. Jackson drove in two runs and then scored the third himself.

As game seven began, Met fans hoped for a repeat of the "miracle" of '69. But Met hopes dimmed when home runs by Campaneris and Jackson helped the A's to an early 4–0 lead and knocked Jon Matlack off the mound. The A's later got another run off reliever Ray Sadecki. The Mets scored just one run in the sixth.

Although the Mets trailed 5–1, they rallied in the ninth, scoring a run and putting two men on base with two out. Met rooters screamed with renewed excitement when Wayne Garrett came to bat—a home run would tie the game. Reliever Darold Knowles, in his seventh Series appearance, forced Garrett to hit a pop fly, and the Oakland Athletics were still the World Champions.

The close pennant races and cliff-hanger Series were only part of the 1973 baseball story, however.

Late in September, Willie Mays announced the end of his 22-year career—a career filled with great plays and great moments. Fans all over the country said a sad goodbye to the "Say Hey" kid.

Another veteran player, Atlanta's Hank Aaron, made happier headlines all summer long, as he crept closer and closer to Babe Ruth's all-time record of 714 career home runs. As the season drew to an end, the countdown began. Aaron collected numbers 710, 711, 712 . . . and finally, number 713—his 40th of the year. But the Hammer was still one away from the magic number. Aaron and his fans eagerly awaited the '74 season when it seemed certain that baseball history would be made.

The game may not have regained its place as America's number one spectator sport, but baseball was obviously still very much alive and doing very well.

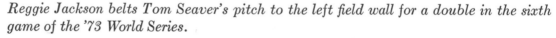

Reggie Jackson belts Tom Seaver's pitch to the left field wall for a double in the sixth game of the '73 World Series.

Baseball's Pennant Winners

Below is a list of pennant winners, beginning in 1901. The number of World Series games won and lost appears after the name of the winner. If no score is given, no Series was played that year.

American League	Year	National League
Chicago	1901	Pittsburgh
Philadelphia	1902	Pittsburgh
Boston 5–3	1903	Pittsburgh
Boston	1904	New York
Philadelphia	1905	New York 4–1
Chicago 4–2	1906	Chicago
Detroit	1907	Chicago 4–0; 1 tie
Detroit	1908	Chicago 4–1
Detroit	1909	Pittsburgh 4–3
Philadelphia 4–1	1910	Chicago
Philadelphia 4–2	1911	New York
Boston 4–3; 1 tie	1912	New York
Philadelphia 4–1	1913	New York
Philadelphia	1914	Boston 4–0
Boston 4–1	1915	Philadelphia
Boston 4–1	1916	Brooklyn
Chicago 4–2	1917	New York
Boston 4–2	1918	Chicago
Chicago	1919	Cincinnati 5–3
Cleveland 5–2	1920	Brooklyn
New York	1921	New York 5–3
New York	1922	New York 4–0; 1 tie
New York 4–2	1923	New York
Washington 4–3	1924	New York
Washington	1925	Pittsburgh 4–3
New York	1926	St. Louis 4–3
New York 4–0	1927	Pittsburgh
New York 4–0	1928	St. Louis
Philadelphia 4–1	1929	Chicago
Philadelphia 4–2	1930	St. Louis
Philadelphia	1931	St. Louis 4–3
New York 4–0	1932	Chicago
Washington	1933	New York 4–1
Detroit	1934	St. Louis 4–3
Detroit 4–2	1935	Chicago
New York 4–2	1936	New York
New York 4–1	1937	New York
New York 4–0	1938	Chicago
New York 4–0	1939	Cincinnati
Detroit	1940	Cincinnati 4–3
New York 4–1	1941	Brooklyn
New York	1942	St. Louis 4–1
New York 4–1	1943	St. Louis

American League	Year	National League
St. Louis	1944	St. Louis 4–2
Detroit 4–3	1945	Chicago
Boston	1946	St. Louis 4–3
New York 4–3	1947	Brooklyn
Cleveland 4–2	1948	Boston
New York 4–1	1949	Brooklyn
New York 4–0	1950	Philadelphia
New York 4–2	1951	New York
New York 4–3	1952	Brooklyn
New York 4–2	1953	Brooklyn
Cleveland	1954	New York 4–0
New York	1955	Brooklyn 4–3
New York 4–3	1956	Brooklyn
New York	1957	Milwaukee 4–3
New York 4–3	1958	Milwaukee
Chicago	1959	Los Angeles 4–2
New York	1960	Pittsburgh 4–3
New York 4–1	1961	Cincinnati
New York 4–3	1962	San Francisco
New York	1963	Los Angeles 4–0
New York	1964	St. Louis 4–3
Minnesota	1965	Los Angeles 4–3
Baltimore 4–0	1966	Los Angeles
Boston	1967	St. Louis 4–3
Detroit 4–3	1968	St. Louis
Baltimore	1969	New York 4–1
Baltimore 4–1	1970	Cincinnati
Baltimore	1971	Pittsburgh 4–3
Oakland 4–3	1972	Cincinnati
Oakland 4–3	1973	New York

Selections made July 21, 1969, in celebration of baseball's 100th birthday.

Greatest Player Ever
Babe Ruth
Greatest Manager Ever
John McGraw
Greatest Living Player
Joe DiMaggio
Greatest Living Manager
Casey Stengel
Greatest Players Ever Team
Babe Ruth, outfield
Joe DiMaggio, outfield
Ty Cobb, outfield
Lou Gehrig, 1st base
Rogers Hornsby, 2nd base
Harold "Pie" Traynor, 3rd base
John "Honus" Wagner, shortstop
Mickey Cochrane, catcher
Walter Johnson, right-hand pitcher
Robert "Lefty" Grove, left-hand pitcher

Greatest Living Players Team
Joe DiMaggio, outfield
Ted Williams, outfield
Willie Mays, outfield
George Sisler and
Stan Musial, 1st base
Charlie Gehringer, 2nd base
Harold "Pie" Traynor, 3rd base
Joe Cronin, shortstop
Bill Dickey, catcher
Bob Feller, right-hand pitcher
Robert "Lefty" Grove, left-hand pitcher

186

Pitchers since 1900 who have won 300 or more games

Denton Young	511	Charles Nichols	360
Walter Johnson	416	Eddie Plank	324
Christy Mathewson	373	Robert Grove	300
Grover Alexander	373	Early Wynn	300
Warren Spahn	363		

Players since 1900 who have hit 300 or more home runs

Babe Ruth	714	Al Kaline	376
Henry Aaron	713	Rocky Colavito	374
Willie Mays	660	Gil Hodges	370
Harmon Killebrew	577	Ralph Kiner	369
Mickey Mantle	536	Joe DiMaggio	361
Jimmy Foxx	534	Frank Howard	360
Frank Robinson	522	Johnny Mize	359
Ted Williams	521	Yogi Berra	358
Ed Mathews	512	Joe Adcock	336
Mel Ott	511	Hank Greenberg	331
Ernie Banks	509	Roy Sievers	318
Lou Gehrig	493	Al Simmons	307
Stan Musial	475	Rogers Hornsby	302
Duke Snider	403	Chuck Klein	300
Willie McCovey	384		

Players since 1900 who have hit .400 or better in one season

Rogers Hornsby	.424 in 1924	Ted Williams	.406 in 1941
Larry Lajoie	.422 in 1901	Rogers Hornsby	.403 in 1925
George Sisler	.420 in 1922	Harry Heilmann	.403 in 1923
Ty Cobb	.420 in 1911	Rogers Hornsby	.401 in 1922
Ty Cobb	.410 in 1912	Bill Terry	.401 in 1930
Joseph Jackson	.408 in 1911	Ty Cobb	.401 in 1922
George Sisler	.407 in 1920		

Players who have hit 50 or more home runs in one season since 1900

162-game season

Roger Maris—61 in 1961   Mickey Mantle—54 in 1961   Willie Mays—52 in 1965

Record for 154-game season

Babe Ruth—60 in 1927	Ralph Kiner—54 in 1949
Babe Ruth—59 in 1921	Mickey Mantle—52 in 1956
Jimmy Foxx—58 in 1932	Ralph Kiner—51 in 1947
Hank Greenberg—58 in 1938	Johnny Mize—51 in 1947
Lewis Wilson—56 in 1930	Willie Mays—51 in 1955
Babe Ruth—54 in 1920	Jimmy Foxx—50 in 1938
Babe Ruth—54 in 1928	

Major League Club Rosters

National League	*American League*
Eastern Division: Chicago Cubs	Eastern Division: Baltimore Orioles
Montreal Expos	Boston Red Sox
New York Mets	Cleveland Indians
Philadelphia Phillies	Detroit Tigers
Pittsburgh Pirates	Milwaukee Brewers
St. Louis Cardinals	New York Yankees
Western Division: Atlanta Braves	Western Division: California Angels
Cincinnati Reds	Chicago White Sox
Houston Astros	Kansas City Royals
Los Angeles Dodgers	Minnesota Twins
San Diego Padres	Oakland Athletics
San Francisco Giants	Texas Rangers

Index

188

hit by Ruth, 74, 75, 76, 81, 85, 87, 88, 89, 90, 97, 101, 104
Hooper, Harry, 64
Hornsby, Rogers, 51, 79, 80, 85, 86, 87, 91, 129, 137
Houk, Ralph, 155, 156
Houston Astros, 150–151, 177
    organized as Colt 45's, 150
Howard, Elston, 142, 153
Hoyt, Waite, 88
Hubbell, Carl Owen, 101, 102, 103
Huggins, Miller, 76, 78, 88
Hulbert, William A., 20, 21, 24, 26
Hunter, Jim ("Catfish"), 169, 183, 184
Huston, Tillinghast L'Hommedieu, 66, 74

Idaho State League, 60
Indianapolis, early teams in, 31, 39, 65
Indians, Cleveland, see Cleveland Indians
International League, 110, 120
Irvin, Monte, 133
Italy, baseball players' tour of, 31

Jackson, Reggie, 179, 184
Jackson, Shoeless Joe, 62, 67, 69, 70
Jansen, Larry, 133
Javier, Julian, 167, 168
Jay, Joey, 147
Jennings, Hugh, 38, 64
Johnson, Bancroft, 39, 40, 41, 48, 64, 71, 77
Johnson, Darrell, 158
Johnson, Walter Perry, 59–60, 62, 64, 81, 82, 106, 169
Jones, Cleon, 5
Jurges, Billy, 94, 95

Kaat, Jim, 166
Kansas City Athletics, 140, 150
    move to Oakland, 152
Kansas City Monarchs, 120
Kansas City Royals, 152
Keane, Johnny, 155–156
Keeler, Wee Willie, 36, 138
Kelly, Michael J., 22, 23, 32, 33, 44
Kelly, Ray, 77
Keltner, Ken, 138
Kerr, Dickie, 67, 69
Killebrew, Harmon, 168
Kinder, Ellis, 129
Kison, Bruce, 177
Knickerbocker Club, 9, 10–12
Knowles, Darold, 184
Knowles, F. M., 43
Koosman, Jerry, 172–173
Kostanty, Jim, 132

Koufax, Sandy, 147, 162–165
Krakauskas, Joe, 138
Kroh, Floyd, 54
Kubek, Tony, 146, 153
Kuhn, Bowie, 170

Labine, Clem, 133
Landis, Kenesaw Mountain, 71, 72, 76, 98
Larsen, Don, 142–144, 145, 167
Latham, Arlie, 23
Lavagetto, Cookie, 123
Lazzeri, Tony, 86, 88, 95
Lemon, Bob, 124, 126, 131, 132
Lewis, Duffy, 64
Lindstrom, Freddy, 81
Lockman, Whitey, 133
Logan, Johnny, 144
Lolich, Mickey, 169–170
Lonborg, Jim, 166, 167, 168
Lopat, Eddie, 130, 131
Los Angeles Angels, 150, 151, 152
    become California Angels, 152
Los Angeles Dodgers, 132–136, 141–142, 145, 147, 149, 155, 158–159, 162–165, 169, 177
Louisville, early teams in, 20, 34, 44
Louisville Eclipse Club, 24

McCarthy, Joe, 90, 111, 113, 130
McCarty's Hotel, 10, 11
McCormick, Mike, 145
McCormick, Moose, 53, 54
McDougald, Gil, 130, 136, 143
McGillicuddy, Cornelius, see Mack, Connie
McGinnity, Joe, 46, 48, 54, 58
McGraw, John, 38, 80, 84, 127, 129, 130
    American League franchise in Baltimore, 41
    first All-Star game, 101
    manager of New York Giants, 46, 48, 58, 76, 78, 79, 101
    with Baltimore Orioles, 36, 37, 38
McInnis, Stuffy, 62
McLain, Denny, 169
Mack, Connie, 40, 41, 46, 47, 50, 65
    first All-Star game, 101
    pennant and 1929 World Series won by, 90–92
McMullin, Fred, 70
McNally, Dave, 173, 174, 176, 177
MacPhail, Larry, 103, 104, 117, 123
Maglie, Sal ("The Barber"), 133, 142
Maharg, Billy, 69, 70
Mantilla, Felix, 144
Mantle, Mickey, 127, 128, 130,

131, 132, 142, 146, 153, 156, 159, 162
Manush, Heinie, 102
Marichal, Juan, 177
Maris, Roger, 153, 157–158, 159, 168
Marquard, Rube, 62, 65
Marshalltown, Iowa, baseball team, 18–19
Martin, Billy, 131, 136
Martin, J. C., 172
Martin, John "Pepper," 92, 93, 94
Martin, Stu, 109
Masi, Phil, 124, 126
Mathews, Ed, 145
Mathewson, Christy, 44, 45, 46, 47, 48, 50, 54, 58, 62, 63, 65
Mathias, Brother, 72
Matlack, Jon, 182, 183, 184
May, Lee, 174
Mays, Willie, 127–128, 129, 161, 177, 179, 184
Mazeroski, Bill, 146, 147
Merkle, Fred, 53, 54, 56, 58
Mets, New York, see New York Mets
Meusel, Bob, 76, 77, 88, 90
Michigan State League, 44
Miljus, John, 90
Millan, Felix, 183
Mills, Abraham G., 7, 8, 26
Mills Commission, 7, 8
Milnar, Al, 138
Milwaukee, early teams in, 39, 41, 47
Milwaukee Braves, 126, 129, 140–142, 144–145, 149, 150
    move to Atlanta, 151–152
Milwaukee Brewers, 152
Minnesota Twins, 149, 151, 163, 165–166, 169, 171, 173
Mitchell, Dale, 143, 144
Montreal Expos, 152
Montreal Royals, 120
Moore, Wiley "Cy," 88
Moose, Bob, 179
Morgan, Joe, 181
Most Valuable Player award, 81, 122
Mountain States League, 110
Mueller, Don, 133
"Murderers' Row," 88
Murphy, Charles Webb, 53
Musial, Stan ("The Man"), 109, 110–111, 120, 124, 160–162
Mutuals, New York, 16

National Association of Professional Base Ball Players, 16, 17, 20
National Commission, 71, 76,
National League, 24, 33, 39, 40, 43, 66, 133, 149, 151, 153, 170
    in All-Star games, 101–103